Slavery, Civil War, and Reconstruction

American History Series

Author:	Cindy Barden
Consultants:	Schyrlet Cameron and Suzanne Myers
Editors:	Mary Dieterich and Sarah M. Anderson
Proofreader:	Margaret Brown

COPYRIGHT © 2011 Mark Twain Media, Inc.

ISBN 978-1-58037-585-6

Printing No. CD-404139

Mark Twain Media, Inc., Publishers
Distributed by Carson-Dellosa Publishing LLC

Visit us at www.carsondellosa.com

Table of Contents

Table of Contents (cont.)

About the American History Series

Slavery, Civil War, and Reconstruction is one of the books in Mark Twain Media's new American History Series. This book focuses on the history of slavery in the United States and how slavery became a social and economic institution. The events that led up to the Civil War are detailed, and Lincoln's presidency during the War is also covered. Students will learn about Reconstruction and how unresolved issues from this period of time impacted later national events. This series is designed to provide students in grades 5 through 8 with opportunities to explore the significant events and people that make up American history. Other books in the series include Exploration, Revolution, and Constitution; Westward Expansion and Migration; and Industrialization Through the Great Depression.

The books in this series are written for classroom teachers, parents, and students. They are designed as stand-alone material for classrooms and home schooling. Also, the books can be used as supplemental material to enhance the history curriculum in the classroom, independent study, or as a tutorial at home.

The text in each book is presented in an easy-to-read format that does not overwhelm the struggling reader. Vocabulary words are boldfaced. Each book provides challenging activities that enable students to explore history, geography, and social studies topics. The activities promote reading, critical thinking, and writing skills. As students learn about the people who influenced history, they will draw conclusions; write opinions; compare and contrast historical events, people, and places; analyze cause and effect; and improve mapping skills. The research and technology activities will further increase their knowledge and understanding of historical events by using reference sources of the Internet.

The easy-to-follow format of the books facilitate planning for the diverse learning styles and skill levels of middle-school students. National standards addressed in each unit are identified and listed at the beginning of the book, simplifying lesson preparation. Each unit provides the teacher with alternative methods of instruction: reading exercises for concept development, simple hands-on activities to strengthen understanding of concepts, and challenging research activities to provide opportunities for students to expand learning. A bibliography of suggested resources is included to assist the teacher in finding additional resources or to provide a list of recommended reading for students who want to expand their knowledge.

The American History Series supports the No Child Left Behind (NCLB) Act. The books promote student knowledge and understanding of history concepts. The content and activities are designed to strengthen the understanding of historical events that have shaped our nation. The units are correlated with the National Standards for United States History (NSH) and Curriculum Standards for Social Studies (NCSS).

Unit Planning Guide

National Standards Matrix

Each unit of study in the book *Slavery, Civil War, and Reconstruction* is designed to strengthen American history literacy skills and are correlated with the National History Standards (NHS) and Curriculum Standards for Social Studies (NCSS).

	Unit 1	Unit 2	Unit 3
National History Standards			
Standard 1: Chronological Thinking	X	X	X
Standard 2: Historical Comprehension	X	X	X
Standard 3: Historical Analysis and Interpretation	X	X	X
Standard 4. Historical Research Capabilities	X	X	X
Curriculum Standards for Social Studies			
Standard 1: Culture	X	X	X
Standard 2: Time, Continuity, and Change	X	X	X
Standard 3: People, Places, and Environments	X	X	X
Standard 4: Individual Development and Identity	X	X	X
Standard 5: Individuals, Groups, and Institutions	X	X	X
Standard 6: Power, Authority, and Governance	X	X	X
Standard 7: Production, Distribution, and Consumption	X	X	X
Standard 8: Science, Technology, and Society	X	X	X
Standard 9: Global Connections	X	X	X
Standard 10: Civil Ideals and Practices	X	X	X

Suggested Resources

Adler, David. *Enemies of Slavery*. New York: Holiday House. 2004.

Allen, Thomas B. *Mr. Lincoln's High-Tech War: How the North Used the Telegraph, Railroads, Surveillance Balloons, Iron-Clads, High-Powered Weapons, and More to Win the Civil War.* Des Moines: National Geographic Children's Books. 2009.

Cloud Tapper, Suzanne. *The Abolition of Slavery: Fighting for a Free America.* Berkeley Heights, NJ: Enslow Publishers. 2007.

De Medeiros, James. *Slavery.* New York: Weigl Publishers Inc. 2009.

Grant, Reg. *Slavery.* London: Dorling Kindersley Limited. 2009.

Greene, Meg. *Into the Land of Freedom: African Americans in Reconstruction.* Minneapolis, MN: Lerner Publications Company. 2004.

Herbert, Janis. *Abraham Lincoln for Kids: His Life and Times with 21 Activities.* Chicago: Chicago Review Press. 2007.

Jordan, Anne Devereaux with Virginia Schomp. *Slavery and Resistance.* Tarrytown, NY: Marshall Cavendish Benchmark. 2007.

Landau, Elaine. *The Emancipation Proclamation: Would You Do What Lincoln Did?* Berkeley Heights, NJ: Enslow Publishers. 2008.

Landau, Elaine. *Fleeing to Freedom on the Underground Railroad: The Courageous Slaves, Agents, and Conductors.* Minneapolis, MN: Twenty-First Century Books. 2006.

Lassieur, Allison. *The Underground Railroad: An Interactive History Adventure.* Mankato, MN: Capstone Press. 2008.

McKissack, Pat. *Days of Jubilee: The End of Slavery in the United States.* New York: Scholastic Press. 2003.

Nardo, Don. *The Atlantic Slave Trade.* Farmington Hills, MI: Lucent Books. 2007.

Osborne, Linda Barrett. *Traveling the Freedom Road: From Slavery & the Civil War Through Reconstruction.* New York: Abrams Books for Young Readers. 2009.

Rappaport, Doreen. *No More! Stories and Songs of Slave Resistance.* Cambridge, MA: Candlewick Press. 2002.

Rossi, Ann. *Freedom Struggle: The Anti-Slavery Movement in America, 1830–1865.* Washington, D.C.: National Geographic Society. 2005.

Schwarz Phillip, ed. *Slavery in the Americas Series.* New York: Facts on File. 2006.

Sharp, S. Pearl with Virginia Schomp. *The Slave Trade and the Middle Passage.* Tarrytown, NY: Marshall Cavendish Benchwork. 2007.

Stein, R. Conrad. *Escaping Slavery on the Underground Railroad.* Berkeley Heights, NJ: Enslow Publishing Inc. 2008.

Sullivan, George. *The Civil War at Sea.* Minneapolis, MN: Twenty-first Century Books. 2001.

Uschan, Michael V. *Reconstruction.* Farmington Hills, MI: Gale. 2008

World Almanac Library of the Civil War Series. Milwaukee, WI: World Almanac Library. 2004.

Slavery Time Line

1619   The first African slaves were brought to Jamestown colony by a Dutch trader.

1634   The first African slaves were imported to Maryland and Massachusetts.

1638   The first American slave auction was held in Jamestown.

1641   The Massachusetts colony legalized slavery.

1642   Virginia law: Anyone who assisted a runaway slave would be fined.

1650   The Connecticut colony legalized slavery.

1661   Virginia legalized slavery.

1662   Virginia law: Any child born of a slave mother would also be a slave.

1663   Maryland law: If a free white woman married a slave, she and their children would be slaves for life.

1681   Maryland law: Children born to free white women and male slaves would be free.

1688   The first formal protest of slavery in the Americas was signed by Pennsylvania Quakers.

1691   Virginia law: Interracial marriage was prohibited.

1776   The Declaration of Independence was signed.

1777   Vermont abolished slavery.

1780   Pennsylvania abolished slavery.

1781   The Massachusetts court awarded freedom to Elizabeth Freeman.

1783   Slavery was abolished in Massachusetts and New Hampshire.

1784   Slavery was abolished in Connecticut and Rhode Island.

1785   New York passed a law against selling any new slaves in the state or selling any New York slaves out of state.

1786   The importation of new slaves ended in all states except Georgia and South Carolina.

1787   Slavery was prohibited in the Northwest Territory.
        The U.S. Constitution was written.

1788   British law restricted the number of slaves carried by a ship, based on the ship's tonnage.

1793   The first federal Fugitive Slave Act made it illegal to assist runaway slaves.

1794   France freed all slaves in the French colonies.

1804   New Jersey abolished slavery.

1807   The British Parliament prohibited British subjects from engaging in the slave trade after March 1, 1808.

1808   The importation of slaves into the United States became illegal.

1817   New York abolished slavery.

1820   The Missouri Compromise was passed to maintain the balance of free and slave states.

1831   William Lloyd Garrison founded the antislavery newspaper, *The Liberator*.

1857   Supreme Court ruled in the *Dred Scott* case.

1860   Abraham Lincoln was elected president.

1861   The Civil War began.

1863   Lincoln issued the Emancipation Proclamation.

1864   President Lincoln was reelected.

1865   The Civil War ended; President Lincoln was assassinated; Andrew Johnson became president; The Thirteenth Amendment abolished slavery in the United States.

Name: _____ Date: _____

Slavery Time Line Activity

Directions: Number the events in order from 1 (first) to 10 (last). Use the time line for reference.

_____ A.   A federal Fugitive Slave Act made it illegal to assist runaway slaves.

_____ B.   Pennsylvania abolished slavery.

_____ C.   The Massachusetts colony legalized slavery.

_____ D.   According to Maryland law, if a free white woman married a slave, she and their

        children would be slaves for life.

_____ E.   Vermont abolished slavery.

_____ F.   Lincoln issued the Emancipation Proclamation.

_____ G.   The importation of slaves into the United States became illegal.

_____ H.   Abraham Lincoln was elected president.

_____ I.   The first slaves were brought to Jamestown colony by a Dutch trader.

_____ J.   The first formal protest of slavery in the Americas was signed by Pennsylvania

        Quakers.

Short Answer: Write the correct answer on the line.

1. Where was the first American slave auction held? _____

2. In what year was Abraham Lincoln assassinated? _____

3. In what year did New Jersey abolish slavery? _____

4. Which state abolished slavery in 1817? _____

5. Which country freed all slaves in their colonies in 1794? _____

6. Who was the founder of the antislavery newspaper, *The Liberator*? _____

7. In what year was the Missouri Compromise passed? _____

8. In 1793, what act made it illegal to assist runaway slaves? _____

9. In what year did the Supreme Court rule on the Dred Scott case? _____

Name: _____ Date: _____

A Historical View of Slavery

Slavery did not begin when the first Dutch ship exchanged a cargo of African slaves for food at the Jamestown colony in 1619, nor did it end when slavery was finally abolished in the United States 246 years later.

Slavery has been part of human history since the earliest times. People in ancient China, India, Mesopotamia, Egypt, Greece, and Rome owned slaves. In South America, the Aztecs, Incas, and Mayas practiced slavery. People in other parts of the world also owned slaves and forced them to work without any pay or **benefits**.

Some people were forced into slavery as a form of punishment because they committed crimes or fell into debt. In these cases, the term of slavery was set for a period of years. After that time, they were again free. The **status** of their children was not affected. Prisoners of war and those kidnapped by pirates became slaves for life. Their children were automatically slaves.

The first known incident of slavery of Africans by Europeans occurred when ten African slaves were kidnapped by a Portuguese trader in 1441 and taken back to Portugal. Kidnapping as a way of obtaining slaves continued for a time, but this soon led to **retribution** by African leaders.

Portuguese traders found they could trade horses, silks, and silver for slaves. Since slavery was common in Africa, leaders saw no reason not to trade slaves for goods with the Europeans. Spain, Portugal, the Netherlands, and other European countries began trading with the people of several great empires (Mali, Benin, Dahomey, and Kongo) along the coast of Africa.

By 1448, there were about a thousand slaves in Portugal, mainly used for **agricultural** work. The Spanish quickly followed the example of the Portuguese, importing slaves to work in their colonies in the New World.

Although slavery is illegal in all countries today, people are still forced into conditions very much like slavery in some countries.

Did You Know?

The first public slave auction in North America was held in Jamestown in 1638.

Name: _____ Date: _____

A Historical View of Slavery (cont.)

Directions: Complete the following exercises.

Matching

_____ 1. slavery

_____ 2. benefits

_____ 3. status

_____ 4. retribution

_____ 5. agriculture

a. pertaining to farming

b. condition or standing at a particular time

c. pay back

d. goods and services offered above wages

e. when a person is considered to be the property of another person

Fill in the Blanks

1. People in ancient China, India, Mesopotamia, Egypt, Greece, and Rome owned

   _____.

2. The first known incident of slavery of Africans by Europeans occurred when _____ African slaves were kidnapped by a _____ trader in 1441 and taken back to

   _____.

3. Portuguese traders found they could trade _____, silks, and

   _____ for slaves.

4. By 1448, there were about a _____ slaves in Portugal, mainly used for agricultural work.

5. The first public slave auction in North America was held in _____ in 1638.

Constructed Response

Directions: Read the statements about conditions in the past. Add a statement about conditions today.

Then: Some people were forced into slavery as a form of punishment or because they could not pay their debts.

Now: _____

_____

Then: Prisoners of war were forced to be slaves.

Now: _____

_____

Then: In 1776, slavery was legal in all states.

Now: _____

_____

Europe and Slavery

Spain and Portugal were the first European nations to engage in the African slave trade. France, Holland, and Denmark also actively bought and sold African slaves. Slaves were taken from Africa to Europe where they were either sold or shipped to the New World for sale.

When Europeans began developing the resources of the Americas, they needed huge amounts of cheap labor. The Spanish and Portuguese forced large numbers of African slaves to work the gold and silver mines and the large sugarcane plantations in Mexico, Central and South America, and the Caribbean Islands.

Not all slaves in the American colonies were Africans. Early in the 1700s, about 25 percent of slaves in colonies such as the Carolinas were Native Americans. From the 1500s through the early 1700s, a small number of white people were also enslaved.

The first African slaves in America were taken to the English colony of Jamestown in 1619. British colonists in both the North and the South owned slaves, but England did not take an active part in **procuring** slaves until after 1650. Eventually the British **dominated** the slave trade.

An Englishman, Sir John Hawkins, came up with the most efficient way of trading African slaves for profit. From England, his ships sailed to the west coast of Africa where they traded goods for slaves. Then they sailed directly to North America where the slaves were sold or exchanged for goods made in the New World. Those goods were taken back to England and sold for a profit.

Soon other European nations followed this **profitable triangular trade route**. The second part of the voyage, from Africa to the Americas, came to be called the **Middle Passage**.

At least 10 million Africans were forced into slavery between the fifteenth and nineteenth centuries. Some scholars estimate even higher numbers.

Did You Know?
The *Clothilde*, the last slave ship, arrived in Mobile, Alabama in 1859.

Name: _____   Date: _____

Europe and Slavery (cont.)

Directions: Complete the following exercises.

Matching

_____ 1. procuring

_____ 2. dominated

_____ 3. profitable

_____ 4. triangular trade route

_____ 5. Middle Passage

a. to make a profit; make money

b. refers to a trade route pattern between England, Africa, and the New World

c. obtaining or acquiring

d. the transportation of slaves from Africa to the Americas

e. to have control over or to rule

Fill in the Blanks

1. _____ and Portugal were the first European nations to engage in the African slave trade.

2. Slaves were taken from Africa to _____ where they were either sold or shipped to the New World for sale.

3. Early in the 1700s, about 25 percent of slaves in colonies such as the Carolinas were _____ Americans.

4. British colonists in both the North and the South owned slaves, but _____ did not take an active part in procuring slaves until after 1650.

5. An Englishman, Sir John _____, came up with the most efficient way of trading African slaves for _____.

Research

Directions: The triangular trade route refers to a pattern of trade between the west coast of Africa, the Americas (both the Colonies and the West Indies) and England. Research the origins of each export item listed below and write on the blank next to it if it was exported from the Americas (AM), England (ENG), or Africa (AF).

1. _____ fish

2. _____ spices

3. _____ sugar

4. _____ teas

5. _____ whale oil

6. _____ tools

7. _____ cloth

8. _____ molasses

9. _____ furniture

10. _____ slaves

11. _____ rum

12. _____ gold

13. _____ lumber

14. _____ pepper

15. _____ tobacco

Life Aboard a Slave Ship

Groups of slaves captured in the **interior** of Africa were forced to march hundreds of miles to the coast. To prevent escape, chains were passed through loops in iron or wooden collars around their necks and through iron cuffs around their wrists and ankles to keep slaves chained together. Often they were forced to carry heavy burdens as they traveled. Any slave attempting to escape would be severely beaten or killed.

When they reached the coast, the slaves were imprisoned until they were sold. The most desirable slaves were males between the ages of 15 and 25. At Fort Elmina in Ghana, up to a thousand slaves could be held in stone dungeons. In Angola, captives were penned in open **stockades**.

After examining the slaves and agreeing on a purchase price, slave traders usually **branded** the slaves with a hot iron to show ownership and returned them to the pens until they had purchased enough slaves to fill their ships.

When they were ready to sail, slave traders herded the captives onto their ships for the five-week journey across the Atlantic. The slaves were crowded into small spaces below deck and were forced to remain there during most of the journey, often chained to each other or to wooden beams.

Water was seldom available for washing. **Ventilation** was poor. Wooden buckets were used as toilets. It was claimed that the odor of a slave ship could be smelled five miles away. Conditions on ships were so dirty, many captives died of diseases. Because of the crowded conditions, diseases often spread quickly.

Slaves were usually brought up on deck and fed twice a day. Meals consisted of **porridge** or beans and water. When the weather was good, slaves might be taken on deck to exercise. This was done to keep the slaves as healthy as possible, because healthy slaves were worth more when sold.

Think About It
Historians estimate that in the late 1600s, about one of every four slaves died while crossing the Atlantic Ocean.

Name: _____ Date: _____

Life Aboard a Slave Ship (cont.)

Directions: Complete the following exercises.

Matching

_____ 1. interior

_____ 2. stockades

_____ 3. branded

_____ 4. ventilation

_____ 5. porridge

a. to be marked with an identifiable symbol

b. exchange of stale or noxious air with fresh air

c. a fenced or enclosed area, such as a fort

d. oatmeal

e. inside; away from the coast

Fill in the Blanks

1. Any slave attempting to escape would be severely _____ or _____.

2. When they reached the coast, the slaves were _____ until they were sold.

3. The most desirable slaves were males between the ages of _____ and _____.

4. When they were ready to sail, slave traders herded the captives onto their ships for the five-week journey across the _____.

5. It was claimed that the odor of a slave ship could be smelled _____ miles away.

Vocabulary

Directions: From the list of words below, select the words that best describe the conditions on a slave ship and write them in the box. Use a dictionary if you are unsure of the meaning of a word.

inhumane	sanitary
adventurous	filthy
gentle	cruel
benevolent	wonderful
terrifying	humane
atrocious	dreadful

Describe the conditions on a slave ship.

Name: _____ Date: _____

What Rights Did Slaves Have?

Each colony enacted its own laws regarding slavery, but by the 1680s, the laws in most colonies were similar. Slavery was legal in all colonies. Slaves were not recognized as persons by law; therefore, they had no legal rights.

Slavery was a permanent condition inherited through the mother. Slaves were considered property. They could be bought, sold, punished, or loaned to someone else in the same way a person might loan a neighbor a shovel or a horse. Like other forms of property, slaves could be passed on to others in a will or given away.

Slaves could not own any property, serve as witnesses in a court, serve on juries, or make contracts. Since marriage is a contract, no slave marriage was considered legal.

Even freed slaves were restricted by laws that controlled their travel, employment, and legal status. In many states, a freed slave was required to leave the state.

Slaves charged with crimes in Virginia were tried in a special court. They had no rights to trial by jury. The purpose of the trial was not to seek justice, but to set an example for other slaves by imposing terrible punishments that could include whipping, branding, hanging, or a tortured death.

Critical Thinking

Which of the rights that you have do you think is the most important? Why? Give specific details or examples to support your answer.

_____

_____

_____

_____

_____

_____

_____

_____

_____

Name: _____ Date: _____

Slavery in the South

Although most people think of white Southerners in the 1700s and 1800s as slave owners, only one in four Southern families actually owned slaves. Three-quarters of Southern families did not own slaves.

Not all blacks in the South were slaves, either. By the time the Civil War began in 1861, about 25 percent of the blacks in the South were free. Most free blacks in the South weren't much better off than slaves, but in some areas they were allowed to marry, own property, attend schools, and even own slaves.

Most movies and books show hundreds of slaves working on huge **plantations**, but that isn't a complete picture. Only about 30,000 Southerners owned 50 or more slaves.

Most Southerners who owned slaves lived and worked on smaller farms and in cities. Slaves not only worked in agriculture, but they also worked in shipyards, businesses, and as house slaves.

Sometimes slaves were hired out by their **masters** and all wages were paid to their owners. Southerners needed cheap labor to work the fields of cotton and tobacco. This made slavery very important to the **economy**.

The invention of the **cotton gin** by Eli Whitney in 1793 cut the cost of producing cotton. This machine could clean cotton much faster than people could. Since this lowered the cost of producing cotton, the price went down, and the demand for cotton cloth increased. Growing more cotton meant the need for even more workers.

Those who owned large plantations and many slaves were from the wealthiest families. They sought to maintain their wealth by controlling the source of their wealth—cotton, slaves, and all laws regarding slavery. Unlike other societies, slavery in the South was not based on forcing prisoners of war to be slaves. Slavery was based on race.

The early European colonists believed that Africans were **inferior**, suited by their character and circumstances to be slaves forever. This attitude remained most strongly in the South, long after Europe abolished slavery and the slave trade.

Name: _____ Date: _____

Slavery in the South (cont.)

Directions: Complete the following exercises.

Matching

_____ 1. plantation
_____ 2. masters
_____ 3. economy
_____ 4. cotton gin
_____ 5. inferior

a. a machine that separates cotton seeds from the cotton
b. a large farm or estate
c. owners of slaves
d. person of lower status
e. production and distribution of goods and services

Fill in the Blanks

1. Three-quarters of _____ families did not own slaves.

2. By the time the Civil War began in 1861, about _____ percent of the blacks in the South were free.

3. Only about 30,000 Southerners owned _____ or more slaves.

4. Southerners needed cheap labor to work the fields of _____ and tobacco.

5. The invention of the cotton gin by _____ - _____ in 1793 cut the cost of producing cotton.

Critical Thinking

How would you feel if you were forced to go to work six days a week for ten or more hours a day but received no pay for your work? Give specific details or examples to support your answer.

_____

_____

_____

_____

_____

_____

_____

_____

_____

_____

Name: _____   Date: _____

Slavery in the North

Slavery was not unique to the Southern colonies. The Dutch imported slaves to New Amsterdam to work on farms in the Hudson River Valley. According to Dutch law, children of freed slaves were still legally slaves.

Other Europeans who settled in the Northern colonies of the New World kept slaves to work in their homes, on farms, and in businesses. Most shipowners and sea captains involved in the slave trade were Northerners. Several Northern coastal cities became centers for slave traffic.

Although never very widespread north of Delaware, slavery did exist in every American colony until the Revolutionary War. Slavery ended in Vermont in 1777. New York was the last Northern state to abolish slavery in 1817.

Even after slavery became illegal in the North, the lives of free blacks were very difficult. Whites, especially recent immigrants, feared blacks would take over jobs, leaving them unemployed. Mobs rampaged through areas where blacks lived and worked in Ohio and New York. Many blacks fled to Canada.

White rioters in Philadelphia in 1834 and 1842 destroyed black churches, attacked black men and women on the streets, and burned their homes. In some states, federal troops were needed to stop the violence.

Schools that allowed black students to attend were destroyed in several Northern states. In Canterbury, Connecticut, a woman named Prudence Crandall ran a private school that admitted black girls in 1833, making it the first integrated classroom in the United States. Shop owners refused to sell her supplies, and neighbors poisoned her well. The town council even passed a law against educating black students from other states in the town. When Crandall persisted, she was arrested. The school building was burned. Crandall was forced to close the school in 1834.

The attitude toward slavery in the North was very mixed. Not every Northerner believed slaves should be free or that blacks deserved equal rights.

Constructed Response

Even after slavery became illegal in the North, the lives of free blacks were very difficult. Why? Give specific details or examples to support your answer.

_____

_____

_____

_____

_____

_____

Name: _____ Date: _____

The Declaration of Independence

When representatives of the American colonies met to form a new nation and declare their freedom from Great Britain, they considered many issues, including slavery.

Thomas Jefferson (a slave owner from Virginia) included ideas from members of the Continental Congress as well as his own ideas about freedom to write the Declaration of Independence. In the first draft, he included a provision that abolished slavery. That section was deleted by the Continental Congress before it was signed in 1776.

The first section of the Declaration of Independence includes these words:

*"We hold these truths to be self-evident, that all men are created equal, that they are endowed by their Creator with certain **unalienable** Rights, that among these are Life, Liberty, and the pursuit of Happiness ..."*

The phrase "all men" did not include African-American or Native American men. The Declaration of Independence also excluded all women of every race and nationality.

The men who signed the Declaration of Independence believed that men had the right to own property. Since slaves were considered property, and property had no rights, there was no reason to include any rights for slaves.

Another section at the beginning of this famous document states that if any form of government does not grant life, liberty, and the pursuit of happiness to the people, they have the right to change or abolish the government and to form a new one that provides for their safety and happiness.

Graphic Organizer

Directions: Complete the vocabulary chart by creating a definition, using the word in a sentence and drawing an illustration that helps you remember the meaning of the word.

Word	Definition	Illustration
unalienable		
	Sentence	

Name: _____ Date: _____

The Constitution of the United States

After the Revolutionary War, the leaders of the new nation met again to write a Constitution in 1787. They did not seriously consider abolishing slavery in the Constitution. If they had, most of the delegates from the Southern states would have refused to sign, and the Southern states would have refused to ratify it.

The delegates felt it was more important to put together a strong new nation than to deal with the difficult and controversial issue of slavery. There were also many other issues besides slavery that needed to be resolved. Many compromises were made before the final draft of the Constitution was approved. Those dealing with slavery were known as the Great Compromise.

Even though the words *slave* and *slavery* do not appear in the Constitution, that document included ten provisions dealing with the issue. In the final version, the United States government could not abolish the importation of new slaves for 20 years, and slave owners had the right to capture runaway slaves, even in Northern states.

Another important issue regarded representation of the states in Congress. Large states wanted more power, based on population. Small states wanted equal representation. In the Constitution, all states received equal representation in the Senate, and the number of members of the House of Representatives was based on population.

This made it necessary for another compromise. Although the Southern states refused to consider blacks as people, they wanted them included in the total population. In the end, it was agreed that for representation in Congress, each slave would be counted as $\frac{3}{5}$ of a person.

States' rights were a major concern, primarily to Southerners who considered belonging to the United States a voluntary agreement. They wanted to limit the power of the federal government. They claimed each state could determine if a federal law was constitutional and could refuse to carry out federal laws if that law infringed on the state's rights.

Critical Thinking

Do you agree or disagree with the decision of the writers of the Constitution in not dealing with the issue of slavery? Give specific details or examples to support your answer.

_____

_____

_____

_____

_____

_____

_____

14

Phillis Wheatley

Phillis Wheatley was captured by slave traders when she was about seven or eight years old. She was taken from Africa in a slave ship in 1761 and sold at an auction. John and Susannah Wheatley of Boston purchased her.

After Phillis learned to speak English, the Wheatleys allowed their daughter Mary to teach her to read and write. They read the Bible and poetry together. Soon Phillis began writing her own poetry.

When Phillis was about 17, Mrs. Wheatley gathered some of her poetry for a book, *Poems on Various Subjects, Religious and Moral,* which was published in England in 1773. The book was very popular, and she was invited to England. Phillis traveled there with the Wheatleys' son, John. In England, she was a popular guest in literary circles.

Phillis stayed in England until she received a letter from Mary Wheatley telling her that Mrs. Wheatley was very ill. Mary asked Phillis to return to Boston. After she returned from England, the Wheatleys set her free. Phillis continued to live with them until Mr. and Mrs. Wheatley died.

"I was treated by her more like her child than her servant," Phillis wrote to a friend after Mrs. Wheatley died.

When the Revolutionary War began, Phillis wrote a poem about George Washington and sent it to him with a letter. Although busy

Phillis Wheatley was the first black woman in America to have her poetry published. She is remembered as "the mother of black literature in America."

with the war, he invited her to visit him at his headquarters in Cambridge, Massachusetts.

Phillis married a free black man, John Peters, but their life was difficult. Because of money problems, John was sent to jail. Phillis had three children, but they all died as babies.

Phillis died on December 5, 1784. Her best-known poems are "To the University of Cambridge in New England" and "To the King's Most Excellent Majesty."

Name: _____ Date: _____

Phillis Wheatley (cont.)

Directions: Complete the following exercises.
Fill in the Blanks

1. Phillis Wheatley was captured by _____ _____ when she was about seven or eight years old.

2. John and Susannah Wheatley of _____ purchased her.

3. After Phillis learned to speak _____, the Wheatleys allowed their daughter Mary to teach her to read and _____.

4. When Phillis was about _____, Mrs. Wheatley gathered some of her poetry for a book, which was published in _____ in 1773.

5. After she returned from England, the Wheatleys set her _____.

Critical Thinking
Directions: Read the following poem by Phillis Wheatley. On the lines below, summarize the meaning of the poem.

On Being Brought From Africa to America

'TWAS mercy brought me from my Pagan land,
Taught my benighted soul to understand
That there's a God, that there's a Saviour too:
Once I redemption neither sought nor knew,
Some view our sable race with scornful eye,
"Their color is a diabolic die."
Remember, Christians, Negroes, black as Cain,
May be refin'd and join the' angelic train.

By Phillis Wheatley
Poems on Various Subjects, Religious and Moral, 1773

_____

_____

_____

_____

_____

_____

_____

UNIT ONE: SLAVERY

Name: _____ Date: _____

The Fugitive Slave Laws

UNIT ONE: SLAVERY

Ever since people were first forced into slavery, they sought ways to escape their **bondage**. In the United States, slaves from Southern states fled to Northern states or to Canada where slavery was illegal. Southerners objected when slaves escaped because they were losing "valuable property."

The **federal** Fugitive Slave Laws in the United States made it easier for slave owners to return runaways back to their homes, even if they were captured in a state where slavery was illegal. These laws reinforced the commitment of the federal government to the belief that slaves were property.

The Fugitive Slave Law of 1793 allowed slave owners or their agents to capture fugitives in any state or territory. "Slave-catchers," professional bounty hunters who hunted for, captured, and returned runaway slaves to their masters, were often **hampered** by whites in Northern cities.

Northerners objected to this law, because they felt it violated civil liberties. As more Northern states abolished slavery, many believed that once a slave entered a free state, he or she should automatically be free. They also felt the law offered too little protection for freed slaves, who were often kidnapped and sold back into slavery.

Slave owners felt the law wasn't strong enough. There were no **penalties** for helping a slave escape or harboring a fugitive. They believed the federal law violated the rights of states to make their own laws regarding property.

The Fugitive Slave Law of 1850 made it **mandatory** for federal marshals to assist in recapturing runaways. It also penalized anyone helping a slave escape; penalties included fines and imprisonment for up to six months.

Fugitive Slaves in the Dismal Swamp, Virginia
by David Edward Cronin

Did You Know?
Henry Brown found a unique way to escape slavery. He had a carpenter build a wooden crate, and he hid inside it. On March 29, 1849, the crate was shipped from Richmond, Virginia, to abolitionists in Philadelphia. Afterward, he was known as Henry Box Brown.

Name: _____ Date: _____

The Fugitive Slave Laws (cont.)

Directions: Complete the following exercises.

Matching

_____ 1. bondage

_____ 2. federal

_____ 3. hampered

_____ 4. penalties

_____ 5. mandatory

a. restricted or prevented

b. national government

c. punishment required by law

d. required by the law

e. slavery

Fill in the Blanks

1. In the United States, slaves from Southern states fled to Northern states or to _____ where slavery was illegal.

2. These laws reinforced the commitment of the federal government to the belief that slaves were _____.

3. The Fugitive Slave Law of _____ allowed slave owners or their agents to capture fugitives in any state or territory.

4. Northerners objected to this law, because they felt it violated _____ _____.

5. The Fugitive Slave Law of 1850 made it mandatory for _____ _____ to assist in recapturing runaways.

Constructed Response

What were two changes made to the Fugitive Slave Law of 1850?

_____

_____

_____

_____

Graphic Organizer

Directions: Take a sheet of paper and make a hot-dog fold. Cut the overlapping section into two flaps. On one flap, write the word **Northerners**. On the other flap, write the word **Southerners**.

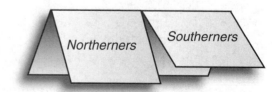

Both Northerners and Southerners had objections to the Fugitive Slave Law of 1793. Under the appropriate flap, write the objections that the group had to this law.

Harriet Beecher Stowe

Harriet Beecher was born on June 14, 1811, in Litchfield, Connecticut. She and her seven brothers and sisters grew up in New England. Their mother died when Harriet was five, so the children were raised by an aunt and a stepmother.

Harriet attended the Hartford Female Seminary, a school run by her sister, Catherine; she later became a teacher there. When her father, a minister, moved to Cincinnati, Ohio, in 1832, Harriet and her sister moved with him. Catherine started another girls' school, and Harriet continued to teach.

Although slavery was not allowed in Ohio, it was legal across the Ohio River in Kentucky. Here Harriet and her family were first exposed to the realities of slavery.

They talked to former slaves and fugitives and heard stories of cruelty and the separation of husbands from wives and parents from children. They read advertisements for the return of runaway slaves and saw slave catchers on the streets.

Harriet married Reverend Calvin Stowe in 1836. When her husband was offered a position at Bowdoin College in Brunswick, Maine, Harriet was glad to leave Cincinnati.

After moving to Maine, Harriet gave birth to her sixth child. The family had little money. Although she had a new baby, four other children, and a home to care for, Harriet helped support her family by writing newspaper and magazine articles. She published her first book, *The Mayflower, or Sketches of Scenes and Characters Among the Descendants of the Pilgrims* in 1843.

Harriet Beecher Stowe

When a black woman hired by the Stowes confessed she was a runaway slave, Harriet and her husband helped her escape to Canada.

Harriet also visited the home of a student, a slave plantation in Kentucky, where she saw slavery firsthand.

When Congress passed the Fugitive Slave Act of 1850, Harriet's sister wrote her: "If I could use a pen as you can, I would write something that will make this nation feel what an accursed thing slavery is."

Harriet decided to write a fictional story about slavery as a serial for an antislavery magazine called the *National Era*. The story, published in 1851 and 1852, grew as she painted a vivid picture of what she had seen and heard about slavery. She wove her story around fictional characters and situations based on real people and experiences.

Name: _____   Date: _____

Harriet Beecher Stowe (cont.)

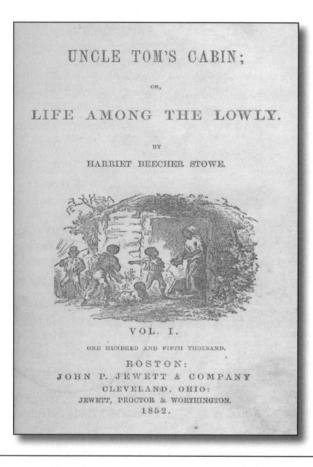

Soon after the serial was complete, it was published as a book.

Harriet hoped to earn a little money from the book to help out her family. The first 5,000 copies sold out in two days. Another 20,000 copies sold in the next three weeks. The publisher couldn't keep up with the demand for copies.

The book was also published in Great Britain and translated into other languages. Although the book was banned in the South, it sold over 500,000 copies in the first five years.

Although it was far from great literature, Harriet's book helped readers see slaves as real people in an unjust and cruel situation. *Uncle Tom's Cabin* drew so much attention and was read by so many people, it may have been one factor that led to the Civil War.

Critical Thinking

If you were able to write a book that would influence people regarding a major issue today, what issue would you write about? Why? Give specific details or examples to support your answer.

_____

_____

_____

_____

_____

_____

_____

_____

_____

Abolitionist Movement

Abolitionists were people who wanted to end slavery. The Society of Friends (Quakers) of Pennsylvania were the earliest group in America to protest slavery. In 1688, four members of the Society of Friends published the first antislavery **resolution** in America.

Many abolitionists believed they could convince others of the evils of slavery by publishing newspapers, almanacs, and books. Abolitionist societies sponsored lectures and invited former slaves like Frederick Douglass and Sojourner Truth to speak at their meetings. They hoped that hearing about the horrors of slavery from people who had been slaves would convince the audience to take action.

> **Did You Know?**
> At their yearly meeting in 1696, the Pennsylvania Quakers agreed to ban the importation of slaves. If a member violated this ban, he or she would be expelled from the group.

In the 1840s, abolitionist societies used songs to stir up enthusiasm at their meetings. To make the songs easier to learn, new words were often set to familiar tunes.

At times, abolitionist speakers found audiences interested in hearing their message. Sometimes, however, the audience responded to those who spoke out against slavery by throwing rotten eggs or rocks. **Elijah Lovejoy**, the publisher of an abolitionist newspaper in Alton, Illinois, was killed by a pro-slavery mob in 1837.

Many abolitionists wanted to end slavery peacefully by legal means through religious and political pressure. They wanted to make people aware of the evils of slavery so that the laws permitting slavery would be repealed.

Even though they wanted to end slavery legally, many became **conductors** on the Underground Railroad, helping runaway slaves escape. Since any assistance of runaway slaves was illegal under the Fugitive Slave Laws, they were technically criminals.

Although many people believed slavery was wrong, they did not believe blacks should have equal rights. They wanted them to be free from slavery, but not to attend the same schools and churches or live in the same neighborhoods as whites. Their solution was to free all slaves and return them to Africa.

William Lloyd Garrison began publishing an antislavery newspaper, **The Liberator**, on January 1, 1831. He also helped form the American Anti-Slavery Society, which tried to coordinate the activities of many local abolitionist societies. In all, about 200,000 people joined the organization.

Although slavery was legal, Garrison felt it was wrong. "That which is not just is not law," he wrote.

The radical tone of *The Liberator* was different from previous abolitionist publications because it labeled slave owners as criminals and called for immediate abolition.

Some abolitionists, like John Brown, believed violence was the only way to end slavery. The actions of the more militant abolitionists brought the issue of slavery to national attention and were another factor contributing to the outbreak of the Civil War.

Name: _____ Date: _____

Abolitionist Movement (cont.)

Directions: Complete the following exercises.
Matching

_____ 1. abolitionists

_____ 2. resolution

_____ 3. Elijah Lovejoy

_____ 4. conductors

_____ 5. *The Liberator*

a. antislavery newspaper

b. statement of beliefs or opinions

c. guides on the Underground Railroad

d. people who actively tried to end slavery

e. newspaper publisher

Fill in the Blanks

1. The Society of Friends (Quakers) of Pennsylvania were the earliest group in _____ to protest slavery.

2. Many abolitionists believed they could convince others of the evils of slavery by publishing _____, almanacs, and _____.

3. In the 1840s, abolitionist societies used _____ to stir up enthusiasm at their meetings.

4. Many abolitionists wanted to end slavery _____ by legal means through religious and political pressure.

5. Although many people believed slavery was wrong, they did not believe blacks should have _____ _____.

Critical Thinking

William Lloyd Garrison wrote, "That which is not just is not law." He believed that though slavery was legal, it was wrong. Do you agree or disagree with Garrison's statement about the law? Give specific details or examples to support your answer.

_____

_____

_____

_____

_____

_____

_____

_____

Name: _____ Date: _____

Nat Turner

From the time he was very young, Nat Turner's mother and other slaves believed he was a prophet with mysterious powers. A popular religious leader and a powerful preacher, Nat strongly believed his purpose in life was to free the slaves. He claimed he heard voices and had visions.

On August 21, 1831, he and five slaves killed their master and his family. They were joined by approximately 60 other slaves from nearby plantations. Nat led the band of slaves against white slave owners, killing more than 50 white men, women, and children.

The group planned to attack the county seat at Jerusalem, Virginia, to obtain supplies and money. However, white militiamen and volunteers attacked and ended the revolt on August 24.

Although many of Nat's men were captured and hanged, Nat escaped to the Great Dismal Swamp where a large group of fugitives lived. There he hid out for several weeks.

Most of Turner's followers were eventually captured, but the hunt for Turner himself went on. Slaves were roughly questioned and their quarters searched.

Born a slave in Southhampton County, Virginia, in 1800, Nat Turner led a rebellion in 1831 that had disastrous consequences.

Finally, Nat surrendered. While a prisoner, he stated: "I had a vision and I saw white spirits and black spirits engaged in battle, and the sun was darkened—the thunder rolled in the heavens, and blood flowed in streams. And I heard a voice saying, 'Such is your luck, such you are called to see; and let it come rough or smooth, you must surely bear it.'"

Nat and others who rebelled were tried in November 1831, convicted, and hanged.

Constructed Response

Why did Nat Turner rebel? Give specific details or examples to support your answer.

_____

_____

_____

_____

_____

_____

_____

Name: _____ Date: _____

The Effects of Turner's Rebellion

As a result of Nat Turner's rebellion, the Virginia legislature debated whether to end slavery, but the movement to abolish slavery, which had gained some support in the South, was almost completely abandoned.

Rather than freeing any slaves, Nat Turner's actions had the opposite effect. In retaliation, whites sought revenge, killing 120 blacks in one day. Most of those were innocent victims who had nothing to do with Turner's rebellion.

Southern legislatures passed stricter controls on slaves. Because Nat Turner could read and write, some slave owners believed that slaves who could read and write were more likely to rebel or run away. Charleston, South Carolina, passed a law forbidding any education for blacks, whether free or slave.

After Turner's rebellion, slaves were forbidden to have any reading materials, even a Bible. They also enforced stricter controls on black preachers, fearing that, like Nat Turner, they would have too much influence on slaves.

Free blacks were not allowed to enter the slave states of Tennessee or Virginia. It was against the law in North Carolina, Mississippi, and Virginia to distribute any antislavery literature.

Some Southern states made it a crime to circulate copies of William Lloyd Garrison's abolitionist newspaper, *The Liberator*, and called for prosecution of Garrison.

In response to actions and stricter controls by whites, more slave revolts occurred in Delaware, Alabama, Kentucky, and Tennessee.

Critical Thinking

Many who believed strongly in abolition felt that violence was the only way to reach their goal of freeing all slaves. Do you agree or disagree? Give specific details or examples to support your answer.

_____

_____

_____

_____

_____

_____

_____

_____

Name: _____   Date: _____

John Brown

John Brown's attempt to end slavery by force at Harpers Ferry increased the tension between the North and South and was another factor contributing to the Civil War.

Born in Connecticut in 1800, John Brown moved with his family to Ohio when he was five. From his father, an active abolitionist, John learned to hate the institution of slavery.

While living in Pennsylvania in 1834, John and other abolitionists began a project to educate black children. In 1855 he joined five of his sons in Kansas Territory in the fight between those who wanted Kansas to be a slave state and those who wanted Kansas to enter the Union as a free state. Throughout his life, he worked for the abolition of slavery.

With financial support from other abolitionists, John began a plan in 1857 to free slaves using a small army. He recruited supporters and established a refuge for fugitive slaves in the mountains of Virginia.

John Brown finally launched his venture on October 16, 1859, with a force of 18 men, including three of his sons. They seized the U.S. arsenal at Harpers Ferry, Virginia, and won control of the town.

They retained control for only a short time, however. In a battle with troops led by Colonel Robert E. Lee, many of Brown's followers and two of his sons were killed. John was wounded and forced to surrender. He was arrested and charged with various crimes, including treason and murder. After being found guilty, John Brown was hanged in Charlestown, Virginia, in December 1859.

For many years, John Brown was regarded by abolitionists as a **martyr** to the cause of human freedom.

Graphic Organizer

Directions: Complete the vocabulary chart by creating a definition, using the word in a sentence and drawing an illustration that helps you remember the meaning of the word.

Word	Definition	Illustration
martyr		
	Sentence	

The Underground Railroad

In spite of the **Fugitive** Slave Laws, slaves still tried to escape, and people helped them by running the Underground Railroad. The **Underground Railroad** was a series of houses, caves, hay mounds, root cellars, attics, chimneys, hidden rooms, sheds, and barns—places where runaway slaves could hide for a short time.

The Underground Railroad also referred to the paths and trails that led from one shelter to the next and to the people, white and black, who helped lead slaves to freedom.

Since it was a secret organization, no one knows for sure how many people became part of the Underground Railroad. John Mason, Josiah Henson, J.W. Loguen, John Parker, and Harriet Tubman were among the more than 500 black conductors on the Underground Railroad.

Most of the first **guides** (later called conductors) on the Underground Railroad were slaves or former slaves. Some secretly helped others to freedom but remained slaves.

Others were freed slaves who put themselves in danger of becoming imprisoned, killed, or enslaved again by helping runaways. Some were slaves who had fled to freedom and then returned to help friends and family members escape.

Along the route to freedom, runaways stayed in **safe houses** and secret hiding places called "stations" and "depots" where they could eat and rest before continuing on their journey.

Some slaves escaped from the South undetected in a wagon with a false bottom. –Photo courtesy Melanie Dobson, author of *Love Finds You in Liberty, Indiana,* a novel of the Civil War.

Many of the first whites who became part of the Underground Railroad were **Quakers**—members of a religious group who strongly opposed slavery.

Other abolitionists in both the North and South helped slaves escape. Although the Fugitive Slave Law of 1850 made it illegal to help runaway slaves, many people ignored the law.

Slave owners feared two things: a major slave uprising and the escape of their slaves. Since a slave could be worth several hundred or even several thousand dollars, a slave who ran away meant an economic loss. They also knew that each slave who escaped encouraged others to try.

Name: _____ Date: _____

The Underground Railroad (cont.)

Directions: Complete the following exercises.

Matching

_____ 1. fugitive

_____ 2. Underground Railroad

_____ 3. guides

_____ 4. safe houses

_____ 5. Quakers

a. secret hiding places called "stations" or "depots"

b. series of places where runaway slaves could hide for a short time

c. members of a religious group who strongly opposed slavery

d. conductors on the Underground Railroad

e. someone illegally "on the run" from the law

Fill in the Blanks

1. The Underground Railroad also referred to the _____ and trails that led from one shelter to the next and to the _____, white and black, who helped lead slaves to freedom.

2. Since it was a _____ organization, no one knows for sure how many people became part of the Underground Railroad.

3. John Mason, Josiah Henson, J.W. Loguen, John Parker, and Harriet Tubman were among the more than 500 _____ conductors on the Underground Railroad.

4. Many of the first whites who became part of the Underground Railroad were _____—members of a religious group who strongly opposed slavery.

5. Although the Fugitive Slave Law of 1850 made it illegal to help _____ _____, many people ignored the law.

Constructed Response

What were two things slave owners feared?

_____

_____

Technology in the Classroom
Primary Source: <http://hdl.loc.gov/loc.rbc/rbpe.08600200>
("$200 reward. Ranaway from the subscriber on the night of Thursday, the 30th of September. Five negro slaves . . . Wm. Russell. St. Louis, Oct. 1, 1847." The Library of Congress American Memory)

Directions: Many people risked their lives to help runaway slaves escape to "free" territories or states on the Underground Railroad. Slave owners offered rewards to slave hunters to find and return runaways. After examining the primary source, create a historical narrative of the escape from the perspective of one of the family members listed on the poster.

UNIT ONE: SLAVERY

Name: _____ Date: _____

Conductors on the Underground Railroad

Men and women were conductors and "station masters" on the Underground Railroad. For blacks, the danger of returning to the South to help others escape was great. If they were free men or women, they could be sold into slavery if caught. Runaways were whipped, beaten, and returned to their masters.

Conductors were both black and white. John Parker was the son of a white man and a slave mother who bought his freedom. From his home in Ripley, Ohio, he rowed across the Ohio River to meet runaways.

Roger Hooker Leavitt used his home in Charlemont, Massachusetts, as a station on the Railroad. One escaped slave named Basil Dorsey lived in Leavitt's home for almost six years in secrecy.

Thomas Garrett was one of the many abolitionists who became conductors on the Underground Railroad. He provided food and shelter to about 2,500 runaways. Finally he was arrested for breaking the Fugitive Slave Law in 1848. The $4,500 fine was so heavy he was forced to sell everything he owned to pay it. In spite of that, he stated, "Friend, I haven't a dollar in the world, but if thee knows a fugitive anywhere on the face of the earth who needs a breakfast, send him to me."

Another abolitionist, Levi Coffin, along with his wife Katie, began helping runaways when he lived in South Carolina. After moving to Newport, Indiana, in 1826, his home became a station on the Railroad. A hundred runaways stopped at his station each year on their way to freedom in Canada. So many slaves passed through his home that it became known as "Grand Central Station" on the Railroad.

A light in the window of Levi Coffin's "station" on the Underground Railroad was always a welcome sight to the weary travelers.

Activity
Directions: Write a windspark poem about the Underground Railroad.

Line 1: I dreamed

Line 2: I was _____. (add a noun)

Line 3: _____ (describe where you were in the dream)

Line 4: _____ (describe an action that took place)

Line 5: _____ (adverb describing how the action was completed)

Name: _____ Date: _____

Harriet Ross Tubman

Slaves called her Moses, because like Moses in the Bible, Harriet Tubman led her people from slavery to freedom.

One of 11 children, Harriet Tubman was born a slave on a Maryland plantation about 1820. She began working when she was six years old and never attended school. Harriet worked as a house servant and in the fields.

When she was 11, Harriet refused to help hold a slave while his owner punished him for trying to escape. The overseer threw a heavy iron weight at the runaway, but it missed and hit Harriet. As a result, she had dizziness and fainting spells for the rest of her life.

In 1844 Harriet married a free black man, John Tubman, but she remained a slave. When Harriet learned that her master planned to sell her, she ran away. Although she was scared, Harriet rode the Underground Railroad to Pennsylvania, where slavery was illegal.

After she was free, Harriet returned secretly to Maryland to rescue family members and many other slaves, leading them all to safety. Harriet later said, "On my Underground Railroad I never ran my train off the track, and I never lost a passenger."

John Tubman refused to join his wife, and he later remarried. Harriet made at least 19 trips, rescuing over 300 slaves, including her parents who were over 70 years old at the time.

Southern plantation owners offered a $40,000 reward for her capture, dead or alive.

During the Civil War, Harriet served the Union Army as a cook, nurse, spy, and scout, but she was never paid for her work. After the war, Harriet married Nelson Davis and bought a home in Auburn, New York.

Harriet helped organize the National Federation of Afro-American Women, opened a home for the aged, assisted the sick and hungry, and helped set up schools for freed slaves. She died on March 10, 1913.

Critical Thinking

Harriet Tubman said, "On my Underground Railroad I never ran my train off the track, and I never lost a passenger." What do you think she meant by this statement? Give specific details or examples to support your answer.

_____

_____

_____

_____

Name: _____   Date: _____

The Missouri Compromise

The Northwest Ordinance of 1787 prohibited slavery in all American territories north and west of the Ohio River. When Missouri applied for statehood in 1819 as a slave state (a state where slavery was legal), many Northerners objected.

At that time there were 11 free states and 11 slave states. By adding another slave state, the balance of power in the Senate would go to those who were for slavery, opening the door for even more slave states to be admitted.

The debate in Congress was long and bitter. Most Northern congressmen refused to accept Missouri as a slave state. They wanted to completely stop the spread of slavery forever, even if they couldn't eliminate it in the South.

Southern congressmen felt that since the Constitution granted the right to own slaves, that right would be taken away if Missouri became a free state, because all slave owners in Missouri would lose their slaves. They felt it was the duty of the federal government to protect private property.

At that time, Maine was not a separate state; it was part of Massachusetts. Maine also applied for statehood. Southern congressmen refused to allow Maine to enter the Union as a free state unless Missouri was allowed to enter as a slave state.

Then Henry Clay created the Missouri Compromise, which was passed by Congress in 1820. Henry Clay was a nationally respected political figure whose genius was in finding a political middle ground when compromise seemed impossible.

The Compromise allowed Missouri to become a slave state and Maine to enter as a free state. In addition, a line was drawn through the Louisiana Purchase at the southern border of Missouri. North of that line (except in Missouri), slavery was prohibited forever.

Many Northerners were unhappy with the compromise because it allowed another state to make slavery legal. Many Southerners were unhappy because they felt they had the right to take their property anywhere in the United States.

Although the Missouri Compromise became a law in 1820, few people on either side of the slavery issue were happy about it.

Critical Thinking

Why do you think Southern Congressmen didn't want Maine to enter as a free state?

_____

_____

_____

_____

Name: _____   Date: _____

The Kansas-Nebraska Act

Slavery became a major issue again when the Nebraska Territory was opened up for settlement. At that time, the area included the modern states of Kansas, Nebraska, and parts of North and South Dakota, Montana, Wyoming, Idaho, and Colorado.

In 1854, Congress passed the Kansas-Nebraska Act, which repealed the section of the Missouri Compromise that banned more slave states north of a line drawn through the Louisiana Purchase at the southern border of Missouri.

One reason for this change was because of the addition of more territory in the Southwest after the Mexican War. This included California, Texas, Nevada, Utah, New Mexico, Arizona, and parts of Idaho, Wyoming, and Colorado.

The Kansas-Nebraska Act allowed inhabitants of each territory to decide for themselves whether they wanted to apply for statehood as a free state or a slave state.

Slave owners in Missouri moved into Kansas with their slaves, hoping to take control

of the area and allow Kansas to be admitted as a slave state. People also moved to Kansas from Iowa and other areas in an attempt to outnumber those who wanted to allow slavery.

Eli Thayer organized the Massachusetts Emigrant Aid Company, which raised money to help settlers from the northeast move to Kansas and to pay for schools, churches, and homes.

Violent battles occurred between pro-slavery settlers and antislavery settlers. The battles turned into a bloody war. Kansas was known for a time as "Bleeding Kansas." Fighting continued for several years, extending the hard feelings that eventually led to the Civil War.

Graphic Organizer
Directions: Learn more about the Kansas-Nebraska Act. On the T-Chart below, write how you think the abolitionists and the slave owners felt about the Kansas-Nebraska Act.

Slave Owners	Abolitionists

The *Dred Scott* Decision

Dred Scott was born a slave in Virginia about 1800. His owner, Peter Blow, moved to St. Louis in 1830 and sold Dred to **John Emerson**, an army surgeon. When Emerson went to Illinois, then to Fort Snelling, an army post in the Wisconsin Territory, he took his slave with him.

While at Fort Snelling, Dred Scott married another slave, **Harriet Robinson**. The Scotts remained at Fort Snelling after Emerson returned to St. Louis and then joined him in 1840.

After Emerson died, Dred Scott went to court to obtain freedom for himself, his wife, and their two daughters. He claimed that because they had lived in a free state and a free **territory**, they had been free, even though they had returned to a slave state. Once free, they should remain free.

Dred Scott was born a slave in Virginia about 1800. The decision made by the Supreme Court in the *Dred Scott* case may have been another factor that contributed to the Civil War.

The St. Louis Circuit Court agreed, but the Missouri Supreme Court reversed the decision, claiming that Missouri would not recognize any federal or state laws that freed slaves. Therefore, the Scotts were slaves and always had been.

Dred Scott **appealed** to the U.S. Supreme Court. In a 7 to 2 decision in 1857, the court decided that Dred Scott was a slave, not a citizen, and therefore not entitled to sue in a federal court.

Chief Justice Taney also claimed that even free blacks were not and could never be U.S. citizens (even though free black men were considered citizens and allowed to vote in several Northern states).

Although the case took several years before a decision was made, both those who were pro-slavery and those who were against it were very interested in hearing the outcome.

Shortly after the Supreme Court decision, the son of Dred Scott's first owner purchased him and his family and set them free.

Although the Dred Scott case had nothing to do with the Missouri Compromise, Chief Justice Taney also declared that the portion of the Missouri Compromise banning slavery north and west of Missouri was **unconstitutional**, because Congress did not have the power to prohibit slavery in federal territories.

Name: _____ Date: _____

The *Dred Scott* Decision (cont.)

Directions: Complete the following exercises.
Matching

_____ 1. John Emerson

_____ 2. Harriet Robinson

_____ 3. territory

_____ 4. appeal

_____ 5. unconstitutional

a. wife of Dred Scott

b. a large tract of land, such as a region, district, etc., that is under a single governing authority

c. not allowed under the Constitution

d. to take a legal case to a higher court for review of a lower court decision

e. army surgeon who bought Dred Scott from Peter Blow

Fill in the Blanks

1. Dred Scott was born a slave in _____ about 1800.

2. After Emerson died, Dred Scott went to court to obtain _____ for himself, his wife, and their two daughters.

3. The St. Louis Circuit Court agreed, but the Missouri _____ _____ reversed the decision, claiming that Missouri would not recognize any federal or state laws that freed slaves.

4. Dred Scott _____ to the U.S. Supreme Court.

5. Chief Justice _____ also claimed that even free blacks were not and could never be U.S. _____.

Critical Thinking

From the perspective of an antislavery or pro-slavery person, write a paragraph on how you feel about the outcome of the *Dred Scott* decision. Give specific details or examples to support your answer.

_____

_____

_____

_____

_____

_____

Name: _____ Date: _____

Sojourner Truth

Born in 1797, her parents named her Isabella. In 1843, she changed her name to Sojourner Truth. Sojourner was sold several times to different masters. When New York passed a law freeing all slaves in the state, her master refused to free her. Taking her infant daughter with her, she ran away to New York City where she found a job as a maid.

Sojourner heard voices she believed to be from God. She began preaching in New York City in 1829. Later she made a lecture tour through Massachusetts, Connecticut, Ohio, Indiana, Illinois, and Kansas.

"I went to the Lord and asked him to give me a new name. And the Lord gave me Sojourner because I was to travel up and down the land showing the people their sins and being a sign unto them. Afterwards, I told the Lord I wanted another name 'cause everybody else had two names; and the Lord gave me Truth, because I was to declare the truth to the people."

Sojourner preached and spoke in favor of the abolitionist movement, becoming the most famous antislavery speaker of the time.

Born a slave in New York about 1797, Sojourner Truth became one of the leading abolitionists as well as an advocate of women's rights.

Although illiterate, she was an effective speaker, and large crowds gathered to listen.

Sojourner was not active in the Underground Railroad, but she inspired many to travel that path to freedom. Attempts were made to stop her from speaking out.

Besides freedom for slaves, she advocated women's rights and a Negro State in the west on public lands.

Graphic Organizer

Directions: Complete the vocabulary chart by creating a definition, using the word in a sentence and drawing an illustration that helps you remember the meaning of the word.

Word	Definition	Illustration
illiterate		
	Sentence	

Name: _____ Date: _____

Frederick Douglass

Frederick Douglass was born a slave about 1817. His owner's wife began teaching him to read and write—until her husband found out. Hugh Auld, like many other slave owners, believed it was more likely for educated slaves to try to escape.

When Hugh Auld died, Frederick went to work as a field hand on Thomas Auld's plantation where slaves were starved, beaten, and forced to work very hard.

When he was 15, Frederick helped organize a Sunday school for slaves that was shut down by angry whites. His master decided Frederick was a troublemaker and sent him to a "slave breaker"—a person who beat disobedient slaves until they were less rebellious. After many beatings, Frederick fought back, and the slave breaker sent him back to his master.

Following an unsuccessful escape, Auld sent Frederick to Baltimore to work in the shipyards. His wages were given to his master.

Frederick Douglass published an antislavery newspaper, *The North Star.* His home in Rochester, New York, became a station on the Underground Railroad.

Disguised as a sailor, Frederick escaped to New York where he married Anna Murray, a free black woman. They moved to New Bedford, Massachusetts.

Invited to talk about his experiences as a slave by the American Anti-Slavery Society, Frederick discovered his true talent as a speaker and leader in the crusade for freedom.

Frederick published *Narrative of the Life of Frederick Douglass, an American Slave*, although friends feared he would be recognized as a runaway slave and recaptured. The book was well-read in the North and Europe. Following a two-year lecture tour in England, Frederick raised enough money to buy his freedom.

Did You Know?

Frederick Douglass was forced to flee to Canada when Virginia issued an arrest warrant charging him with conspiring with John Brown in the raid on Harpers Ferry. Douglass had met Brown and advised him to give up his plan.

Constructed Response

Why didn't slave owners want their slaves to be educated?

_____

_____

_____

Name: _____   Date: _____

Spirituals

Slaves sang as they worked, when they gathered together in the evening, as they rejoiced, and when they were sad. Among the most prominent songs sung by slaves were the spirituals.

Spirituals came from the time of slavery, and their creation ended when slavery ended. The names of those who wrote the words are lost.

Some of the melodies were original. Some were derived from older songs—American, African, and a combination of both.

Nearly 1,000 examples of spirituals have been collected. They are unique in the song literature of the world. It is ironic that one of America's most distinctive contributions to world music is derived from the time when slavery was legal in the United States.

Some spirituals have a religious tone. Many are about the pain and suffering endured by the slaves. Some spirituals speak with longing of a "promised land"—a land where slaves are free.

Technology in the Classroom

Directions: Search the Internet to locate the lyrics of one of the songs listed below. On a separate piece of paper, describe the mood of the song and what the words mean. Give specific details and examples to support your answer.

Blow Your Trumpet, Gabriel	I'm Going Home	Old Ship of Zion
Bound to Go	I'm in Trouble	O Shout Away
Brother, Guide Me Home	In the Mansions Above	Poor Rosy
Brother Moses Gone	I Want to Go Home	Pray On
Build a House in Paradise	Jacob's Ladder	Religion So Sweet
Come Go With Me	Join the Angel Band	Rock O' My Soul
Don't Be Weary, Traveler	Jordan's Mills	Roll, Jordan, Roll
Early in the Morning	Just Now	Shall I Die?
Every Hour in the Day	Lay This Body Down	Shout On, Children
Fare Ye Well	Lonesome Valley	Stars Begin to Fall
Give Up the World	Lord, Remember Me	Travel On
God Got Plenty of Room	Many Thousand Go	Wake Up, Jacob
Go in the Wilderness	Meet, O Lord	What a Trying Time
Good-Bye	Michael, Row the Boat Ashore	We Will March Through the
The Graveyard	My Father, How Long?	Valley
Hallelu, Hallelu	Nobody Knows the Trouble	Winter
Happy Morning	I've Seen	

Name: _____ Date: _____

First Name, Last Name

Directions: Draw lines to match the first names with the last names.

1. ABRAHAM	BROWN
2. DRED	DOUGLASS
3. ELIZABETH	FREEMAN
4. FREDERICK	GARRETT
5. HARRIET	GARRISON
6. JOHN	LINCOLN
7. NAT	SCOTT
8. PHILLIS	TRUTH
9. SOJOURNER	TUBMAN
10. THOMAS	TURNER
11. WILLIAM	WHEATLEY

Directions: Look up, down, backward, forward, and diagonally in the puzzle to find and circle the first and last names of the people listed above.

```
C T W F T T E R R A G K T D T B
V J H B R G U T V Q R S E F W D
W R W K P E B B D M A R X N P O
B V S L Z J D R M M D Y M H Y U
P R P I O P V E O A G N A A L G
Y E R H L W B H R W N X H R T L
X N N K X L T N J I N B A R U A
N R N M D L I K O T C M R I R S
L U T R U T H H T S C K B E N S
O O V C T R H O P M I X A T E F
C J B X Q Y C X R N Q R T Q R J
N O M N F S N R Q G D Y R E K H
I S E L I Z A B E T H V E A T V
L Y E L T A E H W T P M F C G T
W I L L I A M Y R Q A V R N M N
Y X B R B T F N D N Q T A N R M
```

Name: _____ Date: _____

Alike and Different

Directions: Learn more about any two of the people listed. Use the Venn diagram to do a comparison.

John Brown
William Lloyd Garrison
Harriet Beecher Stowe
Sojourner Truth
Dred Scott

Frederick Douglass
Abraham Lincoln
Nat Turner
Harriet Ross Tubman
Phillis Wheatley

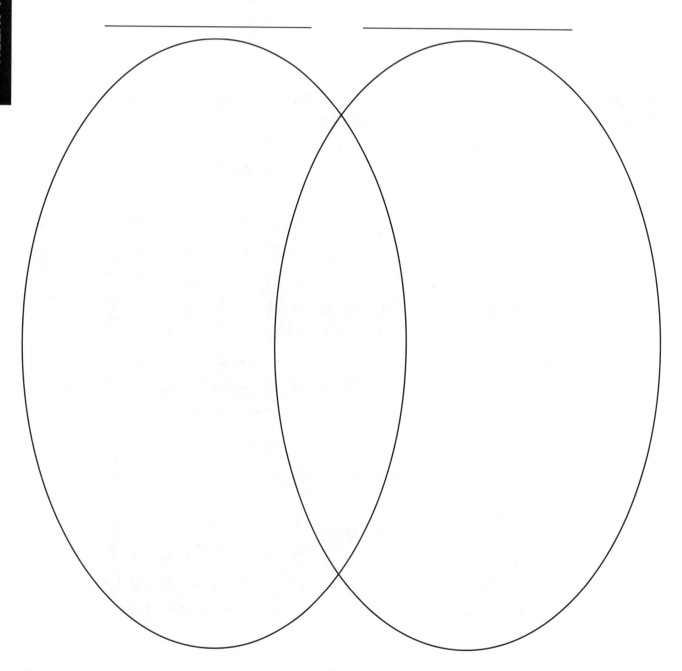

The Civil War Time Line

1619   The first African slaves were brought to Jamestown colony by a Dutch trader.

1688   The first formal protest of slavery in the Americas was signed by Pennsylvania Quakers.

1776   The Declaration of Independence was signed.

1786   Importation of new slaves ended in all states except Georgia and South Carolina.

1787   Slavery was prohibited in the Northwest Territory.

1793   The first federal Fugitive Slave Act made it illegal to assist runaway slaves.

1807   British Parliament prohibited British subjects from engaging in the slave trade after March 1, 1808.

1820   The Missouri Compromise was passed to maintain the balance of free and slave states.

1850   The second Fugitive Slave Law was passed.

1852   *Uncle Tom's Cabin* was published.

1857   The Supreme Court ruled in the *Dred Scott* case.

1860   Abraham Lincoln was elected president.
          South Carolina seceded from the Union.

1861   Mississippi, Florida, Alabama, Georgia, Texas, Virginia, Arkansas, Tennessee, North Carolina, and Louisiana seceded from the Union.
          Kansas was admitted to the Union.
          Jefferson Davis was elected President of the Confederate States of America.
          Abraham Lincoln was inaugurated as president.
          The Battle at Fort Sumter began.
          The First Battle of Bull Run was fought.
          Richmond, Virginia, was named the Confederate capital.

1862   The battle between the U.S.S. *Monitor* and the C.S.S. *Virginia (Merrimac)* took place.
          The Battle of Shiloh was fought.
          Robert E. Lee was appointed commander of the Army of Northern Virginia.
          The Second Battle of Bull Run was fought.
          The Battle of Antietam was fought.

1863   Lincoln issued the Emancipation Proclamation.
          The first Conscription Act was passed.
          The Battle of Chancellorsville was fought.
          The siege of Vicksburg began.
          West Virginia joined the Union as a separate state.
          The Battle of Gettysburg was fought.
          The Confederate fort at Vicksburg was surrendered to Union General Ulysses Grant.
          Lincoln delivered his Gettysburg Address.

1864   Ulysses S. Grant became supreme commander of the Union Army.
          The Battle of Atlanta was fought.
          President Lincoln was reelected.
          William T. Sherman began his march to the sea from Atlanta to Savannah.

1865   The Union Army captured Richmond.
          The Civil War ended when General Lee surrendered.
          President Lincoln was assassinated.
          Andrew Johnson became president.
          The Thirteenth Amendment abolished slavery.

Name: _____ Date: _____

Civil War Time Line Activity

Directions: Number the events in order from 1 (first) to 10 (last). Use the time line for reference.

_____ A. General Lee surrendered at Appomattox Court House.

_____ B. Jefferson Davis was elected president of the Confederacy.

_____ C. Abraham Lincoln was elected president for his first term.

_____ D. The Thirteenth Amendment abolished slavery.

_____ E. South Carolina seceded from the Union.

_____ F. President Lincoln delivered the Gettysburg Address.

_____ G. *Uncle Tom's Cabin* was published.

_____ H. President Lincoln issued the Emancipation Proclamation.

_____ I. President Lincoln was assassinated.

_____ J. The Battle at Fort Sumter was fought.

True or False

Directions: Write "T" if the statement is true or "F" if it is false. Use the time line for reference.

1. T   F   In 1861, Arkansas, Tennessee, North Carolina, and Louisiana seceded from the Union.

2. T   F   In 1863, Jefferson Davis issued the Emancipation Proclamation.

3. T   F   In 1619, the first African slaves were brought to Jamestown colony by a Dutch trader.

4. T   F   The first Conscription Act was passed before Kansas was admitted to the Union.

5. T   F   The First Battle of Bull Run was fought before the Battle at Fort Sumter.

Name: _____ Date: _____

Abraham Lincoln

Abraham Lincoln was born in a log cabin in Kentucky in 1809. His mother died when he was nine. A year later, his father married Sarah Johnston. Although he had less than a year of formal education, Lincoln learned to read and write as a child. His stepmother encouraged him to continue learning on his own.

In 1830, the Lincolns moved to Illinois, were Abe split poles for fences and worked as a store clerk, surveyor, and postmaster. After studying law on his own, Lincoln became a licensed attorney in 1836. He traveled from city to city, often with important papers shoved inside his battered stovepipe hat.

Lincoln was defeated in his first attempt to run for office in 1832, partly because he stopped campaigning to enlist in a volunteer army to put down a Native American rebellion.

His next attempt was successful. Lincoln was elected to the Illinois House of Representatives in 1834, 1836, 1838, and 1840.

Lincoln married Mary Todd in 1842. They had four sons, but only the oldest, Robert Todd Lincoln, lived to adulthood.

Lincoln won the election for U.S. Representative from Illinois in 1846. On many oc-casions, Lincoln clearly stated his belief that slavery was wrong. During a debate about whether Kansas should be a free state or a slave state, Lincoln said:

"It is said that the slaveholder has the same political right to take his Negroes to Kansas that a freeman has to take his hogs or his horses. This would be true if Negroes were property in the same sense that hogs and horses are. But is this the case? It is notoriously not so."

When Lincoln ran against Stephen Douglas in 1858 for the U.S. Senate seat from Illinois, he lost by a narrow margin, but in the presidential election of 1860, he won over Douglas and two other candidates.

By the time Lincoln took office as the sixteenth president on March 4, 1861, seven Southern states had **seceded** from the Union. A month later, the Civil War began.

Lincoln was reelected in 1864 and lived to see the end of the Civil War on April 9, 1865. However, on April 14th, 1865, Lincoln was shot while attending a play at Ford's Theater in Washington, D.C., with his wife and another couple. He died the following day.

UNIT TWO: THE CIVIL WAR

Graphic Organizer
Directions: Complete the vocabulary chart by creating a definition, using the word in a sentence and drawing an illustration that helps you remember the meaning of the word.

Word	Definition	Illustration
seceded		
	Sentence	

Name: _____   Date: _____

Abraham Lincoln (cont.)

Directions: Look up, down, backward, forward, and diagonally in the puzzle to find and circle the words listed below. These words all have to do with Abraham Lincoln and the Civil War.

ABOLITIONIST   APPOMATTOX   ASSASSINATION   BOOTH
CANDIDATE   CONFEDERATE   CONSPIRATOR   DAVIS
DEMOCRATS   DIXIE   ELECTION   ELECTORAL
EMANCIPATION   FUGITIVE   GETTYSBURG   GRANT
LEE   LINCOLN   PRESIDENT   REPUBLICANS
SECESSION   SLAVERY   TYRANT   UNION

```
N E T H P G T Y R A N T K W L C L P
H K L N C G E L E C T I O N N B X N
C L K E A A S S A S S I N A T I O N
A T M L C R U R X K K B H X V M P L
N M Z G M T G N T H L C O M S K K R
D T N E L G O K I E R T F C T H R N
I S O M M S R R I O T Y F L A R E T
D I I A G K I X A A N U C C R N P N
A N S N G Q I V M L G Y O L C B U E
T O S C F D L O A I L L L L O N B D
E I E I T B P Q T D F Y V I M W L I
C T C P W P N I K E R B R N E N I S
W I E A A L V N D E R R O C D E C E
H L S T P E B E V R K T N O R E A R
B O D I R R R A K M G L N L T L N P
P B K O Y A L R X L R L W N P H S R
F A G N T S R O T A R I P S N O C N
C B G E R R G R U B S Y T T E G P M
```

The Election of 1860

By 1860, the nation was divided on the issues of slavery and states' rights. The newly formed **Republican party** nominated Abraham Lincoln as its candidate. Lincoln stated his views on slavery very clearly during his campaign:

"I will not abolish slavery where it already exists, but we must not let the practice spread. I am opposed to allowing slavery in the new territories."

During the campaign, Lincoln was known as "**The Railsplitter**" and "Honest Abe."

Lincoln's political rival, Stephen Douglas, was nominated as the Democratic candidate. Douglas was nicknamed the "**Little Giant**." However, conflict arose between the radical and conservative Democrats.

A separate convention of radical Southern Democrats nominated their own candidate, John C. Breckenridge of Kentucky.

Another group dedicated to keeping the country united formed a new political party, the **Constitutional Unionists**, and nominated John Bell of Tennessee.

With the **Democratic party** split between three candidates, it was doubtful that any of them could win.

To become president, one candidate needed at least 152 electoral votes. When the votes were counted, Lincoln had clearly won.

Lincoln won in most states in the North as well as in California and Oregon. Breckenridge won most states in the South, plus Maryland and Delaware. Bell won in Tennessee, Kentucky, and Virginia.

Although Douglas had the second most popular votes, he only won in Missouri and New Jersey, giving him the lowest number of electoral votes.

UNIT TWO: THE CIVIL WAR

Candidate	Popular Votes	Electoral Votes
Abraham Lincoln	1,766,452	180
Stephen Douglas	1,376,957	12
John C. Breckenridge	849,781	72
John Bell	588,879	39

Name: _____ Date: _____

The Election of 1860 (cont.)

Directions: Complete the following exercises.

Matching

_____ 1. Republican party

_____ 2. "The Railsplitter"

_____ 3. Constitutional Unionists

_____ 4. Democratic party

_____ 5. "Little Giant"

   a. nominated John Bell of Tennessee as its presidential candidate

   b. split between three candidates

   c. nickname for Abraham Lincoln

   d. nickname for Stephen Douglas

   e. nominated Abraham Lincoln as its presidential candidate

Fill in the Blanks

1. By 1860, the nation was divided on the issues of _____ and _____ rights.

2. The newly formed Republican party nominated _____ _____ as its candidate

3. Lincoln's political rival, _____ _____, was nominated as the Democratic candidate

4. A separate convention of _____ Southern _____ nominated their own candidate, John C. Breckenridge of Kentucky.

5. Another group dedicated to keeping the country united formed a new political party, the _____ _____, and nominated John Bell of Tennessee.

Chart

Directions: To become president, a candidate needed at least 152 electoral votes. Use the chart to answer the questions about the 1860 election below.

Candidate	Popular Votes	Electoral Votes
Abraham Lincoln	1,766,452	180
Stephen Douglas	1,376,957	12
John C. Breckenridge	849,781	72
John Bell	588,879	39

1. How many votes were cast in the election? _____
2. What percent of the total votes did Lincoln receive? _____
3. What percent of the total votes did Douglas receive? _____
4. What percent of the electoral votes did Lincoln receive? _____
5. What percent of the electoral votes did Douglas receive? _____

Name: _____ Date: _____

Election Results

Electoral votes are based on the population of each state. The candidate who gets the most popular votes in a state usually receives all the electoral votes for that state.

Directions: Complete the map below.

1. In the 1860 presidential election, the border candidate, John Bell, won in Tennessee, Kentucky, and Virginia. Color those states green.

2. Lincoln won in most states in the North as well as in California and Oregon. Color those states blue.

3. Breckenridge won the electoral votes in most states in the South, plus Maryland and Delaware. Color those states grey.

4. Although Douglas had the second most popular votes, he only won enough popular votes in Missouri and New Jersey to earn any electoral votes. Color Missouri and New Jersey red.

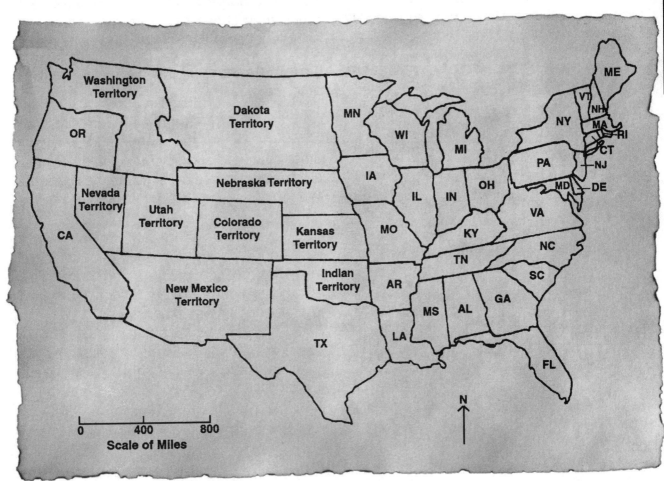

Causes of the Civil War

By the time Lincoln was elected president in November 1860, the Civil War was so close to beginning that it was unlikely that anyone could have prevented it. Before he even officially became president in March 1861, seven states had seceded from the Union, and Jefferson Davis had already been elected President of the Confederate States of America.

What caused the Civil War? The disagreement about slavery was probably the major cause. Although there were many differences between the Southern and Northern states, slavery was the only institution not shared by both areas.

Besides the disagreement between the North and South about the legality and morality of slavery, there were other causes.

The Expansion of Slavery:

Northerners wanted to end the expansion of slavery. Slave owners wanted to extend slavery to all new states.

States' Rights:

Southerners believed individual states should have more control over laws than the federal government. Northerners felt the federal government should have more power than any individual state.

The Union:

Northerners believed the United States must remain one country to remain strong. Southerners claimed that the United States was an organization of independent states. Since they chose to join it, they could also choose to leave it and form their own country.

Tariffs: (taxes on goods brought in from another country)

Southern farmers and plantation owners wanted to sell their cotton and tobacco to other countries and buy manufactured goods as cheaply as possible because the South had few factories. They did not want to pay tariffs.

Northern factory owners wanted high tariffs on imported goods so they could sell their own products in the United States. They wanted to keep out competition by making foreign goods more expensive.

Name: _____ Date: _____

Causes of the Civil War (cont.)

Graphic Organizer
Directions: Besides the disagreement between the North and South about the legality and morality of slavery, there were other causes for the Civil War. Complete the chart below by writing the position taken by each side on the issues listed below.

Issue	North	South
The Expansion of Slavery		
States' Rights		
The Union		
Tariffs		

CD-404139 © Mark Twain Media, Inc., Publishers   47

Name: _____ Date: _____

Secession Divides the Nation

When Abraham Lincoln was elected president in November 1860, there were 33 states in the Union. By the time he took office in March 1861, seven states had decided they no longer wanted to be part of the United States.

South Carolina seceded from the United States in December 1860. The following year Alabama, Arkansas, Florida, Georgia, Louisiana, Mississippi, North Carolina, Tennessee, Texas, and Virginia joined South Carolina to form the Confederate States of America. They elected Jefferson Davis as their new president.

Their argument was that the Union was an organization of independent states. Since they chose to join it, they could also choose to leave it.

When the North refused to accept their decision, the Southern States regarded the Civil War as the second war of independence.

When the Civil War began, slavery was legal in four border states: Delaware, Maryland, Kentucky, and Missouri. It was even legal in the nation's capital, Washington, D.C.

For a time, it was uncertain what would happen in the border states between the North and South. Although the South expected Kentucky and Missouri to join the Confederacy, in the end all four states remained with the Union.

Kansas joined the Union as a state in January 1861, and part of Virginia separated from the rest of the state and became West Virginia, a Union state in 1863.

UNIT TWO: THE CIVIL WAR

Research

Directions: When the Civil War began, the first official confederate flag was called the "Stars and Bars." Many people thought it looked too similar to the "Stars and Stripes," the official United States flag. On May 1, 1863, the Confederacy adopted a new design for the Confederate flag. Learn more about the flags of the Civil War, then draw and color each of the flags.

Stars and Stripes

Stars and Bars

Jefferson Davis

The youngest of ten children, Jefferson Davis was born in Kentucky in 1808 and moved with his family to Mississippi two years later. His father, a farmer, worked along with his slaves to clear the land and plant cotton.

Davis attended the Transylvania University in Kentucky and the U.S. Military Academy at West Point. He graduated 23rd out of 32 in 1828. Davis served at frontier outposts in the Wisconsin and Michigan Territories. There, he met and fell in love with Sarah Knox Taylor, the daughter of Zachary Taylor.

After their marriage in June 1835, Davis resigned his army commission and moved to Mississippi. His wife died of malaria three months after their wedding.

Davis married 19-year-old Varina Howell in 1845. That same year, he was elected to Congress. The Mexican War began before he completed his first term. Elected colonel by a regiment of Mississippi volunteers, Davis led his troops to Mexico.

After being wounded in the foot by a bullet in 1847, Davis was appointed by the governor of Mississippi to finish out the term of a U.S. senator who had died. He served in the Senate until 1850.

President Pierce appointed Davis as Secretary of War in 1853. Davis increased the size of the army, ordered improvements in uniforms and equipment, and introduced the military use of camels in the deserts of the West.

Davis returned to the Senate in 1857 but resigned on January 21, 1861, after seven Southern states seceded from the Union.

Jefferson Davis

Davis was unanimously elected as President of the Confederate States of America by Southern leaders in Montgomery, Alabama. His first official act was to send a peace commission to Washington in an attempt to avoid armed conflict.

When General Robert E. Lee surrendered at the end of the Civil War, Davis fled to Georgia where he was captured by Union troops.

He spent nearly two years in prison because he refused to take an oath of allegiance to the United States. He was finally released after several Northerners raised the $100,000 needed for bail.

Davis lived in Canada and Europe for a time. He died in New Orleans on December 6, 1889, at the age of 81.

Name: _____   Date: _____

Jefferson Davis (cont.)

Comprehension

Directions: Circle the word or phrase that makes each sentence about Jefferson Davis true.

1. The youngest of ten children, Jefferson Davis was born in (Alabama / Kentucky) in 1808.

2. He moved with his family to (Mississippi / Virginia) two years later. His father, a farmer, worked along with his slaves to clear the land and plant cotton

3. Davis attended (Harvard Law School / Transylvania University in Kentucky) and the U.S. Military Academy at West Point. He graduated 23rd out of 32 in 1828.

4. Davis served at frontier outposts in the Wisconsin and Michigan Territories. There, he met and fell in love with Sarah Knox Taylor, the daughter of (Zachary Taylor / Ulysses S. Grant).

5. After their marriage in June 1835, Davis resigned his army commission and moved to (Georgia / Mississippi). His wife died of malaria three months after their wedding.

6. Davis married 19-year-old Varina Howell in 1845. That same year, he was elected (to Congress / as governor of Alabama).

7. After being wounded in the (foot / eye) by a bullet in 1847, Davis was appointed by the governor of Mississippi to finish out the term of a U.S. senator who had died. He served in the Senate until 1850.

8. President Pierce appointed Davis as (Secretary of War / Secretary of State) in 1853.

9. Davis increased the size of the army, ordered improvements in uniforms and equipment, and introduced the military use of (elephants / camels) in the deserts of the West.

10. Davis returned to the Senate in 1857 but resigned on January 21, 1861, after seven Southern states seceded from the Union. Davis was unanimously elected as President of the Confederate States of America by Southern leaders in (Richmond, Virginia / Montgomery, Alabama).

11. When General (Robert E. Lee / Ulysses S. Grant) surrendered at the end of the Civil War, Davis fled to Georgia where he was captured by Union troops. He spent nearly two years in prison because he refused to take an oath of allegiance to the United States.

12. He was finally released after several (Northerners / Southerners) raised the $100,000 needed for bail.

Name: _____ Date: _____

Abraham Lincoln or Jefferson Davis?

During the Civil War, Abraham Lincoln and Jefferson Davis were prominent leaders. Abraham Lincoln was President of the United States of America. Jefferson Davis was President of the Confederate States of America.

Research
Directions: Learn more about Abraham Lincoln and Jefferson Davis. Write "AL" on the blank if the statement refers to Abraham Lincoln. Write "JD" if it refers to Jefferson Davis. Wrote "Both" if the statement refers to both men.

_____ 1. He was born in 1808.

_____ 2. He was born in Kentucky.

_____ 3. He was a lawyer.

_____ 4. He married Mary Todd.

_____ 5. He had four sons; three of them died before becoming adults.

_____ 6. He served as Secretary of War when Franklin Pierce was president.

_____ 7. He attended Transylvania University.

_____ 8. He served in the U.S. Congress.

_____ 9. His father, Thomas, was a carpenter.

_____ 10. He attended West Point Military Academy.

_____ 11. He was appointed postmaster of new Salem and worked as the deputy surveyor of Sangamon County.

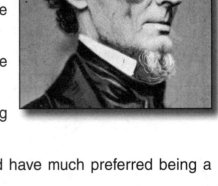

_____ 12. His wife died three months after they were married.

_____ 13. His career included terms in both the House and the Senate.

_____ 14. Many citizens accused him of not doing everything possible to end the war.

_____ 15. He did not care to be president; he would have much preferred being a general.

Name: _____   Date: _____

The War Begins

When Jefferson Davis became President of the Confederacy, he ordered all federal troops to leave all government forts and buildings in Confederate territory. Abraham Lincoln refused to comply with this order and pledged to maintain control of all federal property.

The Confederates demanded that Major Robert Anderson surrender Fort Sumter off the coast of South Carolina; he refused. On April 12, 1861, Confederate troops fired on Fort Sumter. Two days later, Major Anderson surrendered. President Lincoln immediately called for 75,000 army volunteers and declared a naval blockade of all Southern ports.

Learning that a battle would soon take place at Bull Run near Manassas, Virginia, 35 miles south of Washington, D.C., hundreds of curious men, women, and children followed the Union soldiers to the battlefield on July 21,

1861. They drove fancy carriages and brought along picnic lunches, champagne, and blankets to sit on while they watched the battle.

As the Confederate troops headed toward Bull Run, Southern women threw flowers to their soldiers and served lemonade. Soldiers smiled and laughed as they marched.

Suddenly, guns and cannons roared. The picnic was over. Soldiers were wounded and killed. At first, it seemed that the Union troops would win, but when Confederate reinforcements arrived, the Union soldiers panicked and began a disorderly retreat.

When the sightseers realized what was happening, they ran, too. The onlookers found themselves in the midst of chaos as soldiers and civilians crowded the road back to Washington. Wounded men, army wagons, and ambulances surrounded the fancy carriages.

It took two days for all the Union soldiers to straggle back to the capital. The people of the city were terrified. If the Confederate Army had continued to pursue the Union Troops, they may have been able to capture Washington, D.C., easily. Instead, they returned to the South and celebrated their victory.

Critical Thinking

Why do you think the people treated the battle as entertainment? Give specific details or examples to support your answer.

_____

_____

_____

_____

Name: _____ Date: _____

Who Started the Civil War?

The South:
- Fired the first shots at Fort Sumter.
- Seceded from the Union.
- Refused to abolish slavery.
- Insisted on states' rights over the federal government.
- Attempted to make slavery legal in new states.

The North:
- Refused to let the Southern states form their own country.
- Tried to force the South to abolish slavery.
- Put economic pressure on the South.
- Tried to prevent slavery from spreading to new states.
- Helped slaves escape, even though it was illegal.

Conditions causing the Civil War began long before the first shots were fired at Fort Sumter or when Abraham Lincoln was elected president and South Carolina decided to leave the Union.

Many compromises had been tried to iron out the differences between the North and the South from the time the U.S. Constitution was written. Some worked for a while, but in the end, they all failed.

While in Congress, Lincoln proposed an emancipation program to free all slaves born after January 1, 1850, and enroll them in an apprenticeship program. He proposed that emancipation of current slaves would be voluntary, and anyone who freed his slaves would be compensated by the government.

His proposal and others for eliminating slavery gradually to avoid extreme economic hardship on Southern slaveholders were not accepted.

Cause and Effect
Directions: A **cause** is an event that produces a result. An **effect** is the result produced. For each statement below, write a cause or effect.

1. **Cause:** Abraham Lincoln was elected president.

   Effect: _____

   _____

2. **Cause:** _____

   _____

   Effect: Many Northerners helped slaves escape, even though it was illegal.

Name: _____ Date: _____

Lincoln's Views on Slavery

Abraham Lincoln, the sixteenth President of the United States, is well known for his famous Gettysburg Address, a speech he gave at the Gettysburg battlefield during the Civil War. He began the Gettysburg Address by saying:

"Four score and seven years ago, our fathers brought forth on this continent, a new nation, conceived in Liberty, and dedicated to the proposition that all men are created equal."

On many occasions, Lincoln clearly stated his belief that slavery was wrong and that all men were created equal.

Critical Thinking

Directions: Read the words of Abraham Lincoln below. Under the quote, write your opinion of what he said. Explain what you think he meant. Give specific details or examples to support your opinion. Use your own paper if you need more room.

1. During a debate about whether Kansas should be a free state or a slave state, Lincoln said:

"It is said that the slaveholder has the same political right to take his Negroes to Kansas that a freeman has to take his hogs or his horses. This would be true if Negroes were property in the same sense that hogs and horses are. But is this the case? It is notoriously not so."

_____

_____

_____

_____

_____

2. Lincoln was referring to the Declaration of Independence , which states that " . . . all men are created equal . . ." when he spoke these words:

"Let us discard all this quibbling about this man and that man—this race and the other race being inferior, and therefore they must be placed in an inferior position. Let us discard all these things, and unite as one people throughout the land, until we shall once more stand up declaring that all men are created equal."

_____

_____

_____

_____

_____

Name: _____   Date: _____

Grant or Lee?

Robert E. Lee and Ulysses S. Grant were famous generals during the Civil War. One led the Union Army. The other led the Confederate Army. One accepted the surrender of the other at Appomattox Court House, Virginia.

Research

Directions: Learn more about Lee and Grant. Write "LEE" on the blank if the statement refers to Robert E. Lee. Write "GRANT" if it refers to Ulysses S. Grant.

_____ 1. He was born in 1807 on a plantation on the banks of the Potomac River.

_____ 2. He was born in 1822 in a two-room log cabin in Ohio.

_____ 3. His father was a tanner.

_____ 4. His father had been a hero in the Revolutionary War.

_____ 5. His family moved to Georgetown, Ohio, when he was a year old.

_____ 6. When he was three years old, his father made many bad investments and was sent to debtors' prison.

_____ 7. He graduated 2nd highest in his class of 46 from the U.S. Military Academy at West Point.

_____ 8. He graduated 21st in a class of 39 from the U.S. Military Academy at West Point.

_____ 9. He married Julia Dent.

_____ 10. He married Mary Anne Randolph Custis, the great-great-granddaughter of Martha Washington.

_____ 11. He served three years as superintendent of the U.S. Military Academy while his son was a cadet there.

_____ 12. He was forced to resign from the army because of his heavy drinking and quarrels with his commander.

_____ 13. He built a log cabin for his family in Missouri and farmed for a while.

_____ 14. After the Civil War, he became president of Washington College in Lexington, Virginia.

_____ 15. After the Civil War, he served two terms as President of the United States.

The Glories of War

Being a soldier during the Civil War must have been a wonderful experience, right? Not necessarily. First and foremost, thousands of soldiers died.

At the battle of Bull Run, 5,000 soldiers died. During the Battle of Spotsylvania, 12,000 men were killed in one day. By the time the war was over, 620,000 Americans were dead.

Those who lived through battles saw acre after acre of mutilated bodies. Friends and family members died. Streams and creeks ran red with blood. At times, there were too many dead to bury them all.

Thousands of soldiers were wounded. Conditions in army hospitals were terrible. There were few doctors and nurses, no antibiotics, and no anesthetics. Many wounds became infected.

Think About It

General Stonewall Jackson is buried in two places. His left arm was amputated after the Battle of Chancellorsville in 1863 and buried on a nearby farm. When he died a week later, Jackson was buried in Lexington, Virginia.

If an arm or leg needed to be amputated, several people held the patient while the surgeon cut the limb off with a saw. Those who were lucky passed out from the pain. Even those who weren't wounded might contract a disease that could be fatal, such as typhoid.

For every man in the Confederate Army who died in battle, three died from disease. Conditions in the Union Army were almost as bad.

Sometimes food was scarce, or what was available was moldy or full of bugs. Soldiers walked so many miles that they wore their boots out. Then they simply wrapped rags around their feet and kept going.

Men were often scared or homesick. They missed parents, children, and wives or sweethearts. Conditions in the camps were filthy. Bathrooms were open trenches dug in the ground.

In winter, wood wasn't always available to use for cooking and keeping warm. Tents offered little shelter from snow and wind.

In the summer, heat took its toll on men marching for long distances, especially when drinking water was scarce. Keeping clean was nearly impossible most of the time. Lice and bedbugs plagued the soldiers. Rain might bring relief from the heat, but it also meant walking and sleeping in mud.

When you see photos of men happily marching off to war, remember that being a solider in the Civil War wasn't really such a wonderful experience after all. In spite of that, many brave soldiers did what they considered their duty: to fight for the cause they thought was right.

Name: _____ Date: _____

The Glories of War (cont.)

Research
Directions: By the time the Civil War was over, 620,000 Americans were dead. Learn more about each battle listed below. Use the information you find to complete the chart below.

Battle	Date	State	Casualties
Antietam			
Fort Sumter			
The First Battle of Bull Run			
Battle of Fredericksburg			
Battle of Gettysburg			
Battle of Lookout Mountain			
Battle of Murfreesboro			
Battle of Pea Ridge			
Battle of Shiloh			
Siege of Vicksburg			

UNIT TWO: THE CIVIL WAR

Name: _____ Date: _____

What Did They Wear?

When people think of soldiers in the Civil War, they often think of Union troops in blue and Confederate troops in gray uniforms. Sometimes, that was not the case.

Both the Northern and Southern armies were made up mostly of volunteers. Some volunteer groups had their own uniforms that were completely different from the standard.

The New York 79th Infantry soldiers (Union Highlanders) wore kilts to battle, while the Confederate Louisiana Tiger Zouaves wore a short gold jacket, wide trousers, and a red cap.

Directions: Use the key at the right to color the standard uniforms of the Union and Confederate Armies.

A. Tan	B. Gray	C. Light Blue
D. Dark Blue	E. Yellow	F. Black
G. Brown		

Union Standard Uniform   **Confederate Standard Uniform**

Name: _____ Date: _____

The First Air Corps

In 1861, 42 years before the Wright brothers made their first airplane flight, President Lincoln named Thaddeus Lowe Chief Aeronaut of the Army of the Potomac. What was an **aeronaut**? At that time, it was a person who flew in a hot air balloon.

Lowe recruited and managed the North's first **hot air balloon corps**, which provided aerial surveillance during the first two years of the Civil War. He and his airship crew made over 3,000 flights into Confederate territory.

On August 3, 1861, the **U.S.S.** *Fanny* became the country's first aircraft carrier. Aeronaut John LaMountain used the ship as a base for a balloon survey of Southern activities along the Potomac River. From the air, he could get a better view of the scene below, including numbers and placement of troops.

Confederate General James Longstreet remarked, "The Federals had been using balloons in examining our positions, and we watched with envious eyes their beautiful observation as they floated high in the air, well out of range of our guns."

The first Confederate balloons were made of varnished cotton and inflated with air heated by burning pine knots and turpentine.

These were tethered to half-mile ropes connected to a windlass.

Cotton was not satisfactory material for hot air balloons, but the cost of silk, the best material, was too expensive. The Confederates overcame this problem by sewing together pieces of silk from dresses donated by Southern women to make a balloon.

At the Battle of Fair Oaks in May 1862, Lowe's observations from a hydrogen balloon provided vital information that narrowly averted a Union defeat, according to his unpublished memoirs.

Despite the advantage of air surveillance, many Union generals were not convinced of its value, and the air corps was expensive to maintain. When Lowe quit in 1863, the air corps itself was discontinued.

UNIT TWO: THE CIVIL WAR

Critical Thinking

How do you think the use of hot air balloons gave the North an advantage? Give specific details or examples to support your answer.

_____

_____

_____

_____

The War at Sea

Except for a few gunboats at the beginning of the Civil War, the South had no ships to protect its 3,500-mile coastline from Virginia to Texas.

Union ships patrolled the Atlantic coast and the Gulf of Mexico, blocking Confederate trade routes. This prevented the South from receiving supplies or sending cotton, tobacco, and other trade goods to be sold.

Stephen Mallory, Confederate Secretary of the Navy, decided the South needed an ironclad ship. They raised the **U.S.S. *Merrimac*,** which had been sunk at the beginning of the war to prevent it from falling into Confederate hands. They covered the ship with iron plating and renamed it the **C.S.S. *Virginia*.**

When the North learned about the C.S.S. *Virginia*, they decided to build their own ironclad ship, the **U.S.S. *Monitor*.** By then, though, the South had a three-month head start.

Both navies rushed to complete their ships. Many people expected the **ironclads** to sink as soon as they were launched. They didn't sink, but both had serious problems and there was no time to fix everything.

In its first battle at Hampton Roads on March 8, 1862, the *Virginia* destroyed two Union warships, caused one to become grounded, and drove off two others.

The *Monitor* arrived the following day, before the *Virginia* could destroy the ship that had run aground. Only 50 yards apart at times, the two ironclads blasted cannonballs at each other.

The *Virginia (Merrimac)* on the left is approached by the *Monitor* on the right.

Both crews fought desperately to keep their ships afloat. When cannonballs failed to sink the *Monitor*, the *Virginia* tried to ram the ship, but missed by a few feet. After a four-hour battle, the *Monitor* headed for water too shallow for the *Virginia* to follow.

The *Virginia* returned to port for repairs, where they discovered the ship had been hit by cannonballs at least 150 times during its two-day battle. The *Monitor* had been hit 23 times.

After being repaired, the *Virginia* returned to Hampton Roads on April 11, where the *Monitor* and a pack of Union warships waited. Outnumbered and surrounded, the crew set fire to the *Virginia*. It burned until it finally exploded. The *Monitor* later sank in a December storm.

The South built 22 ironclad ships, but the North built more than 60. With their superior numbers, the Union tightened the blockade, captured most of the major ports in the South, and controlled the rivers.

Name: _____ Date: _____

The War at Sea (cont.)

True or False
Directions: Write "T" if the statement is true or "F" if it is false.

1.　T　　F　　Stephen Mallory, Confederate Secretary of the Navy, decided the South needed an ironclad ship.

2.　T　　F　　The South decided to build the ironclad ship, the U.S.S. *Monitor*.

3.　T　　F　　The U.S.S. *Merrimac* was covered with iron plating and renamed the C.S.S. *Virginia*.

4.　T　　F　　The North built 22 ironclad ships, but the South built more than 60.

5.　T　　F　　With their superior ironclad ship numbers, the Confederates captured most of the major ports in the North and controlled the rivers.

6.　T　　F　　At Hampton Roads on April 11, the *Virginia* was destroyed by its own crew.

7.　T　　F　　The *Monitor* sank in a December storm.

8.　T　　F　　Many people expected the ironclads to sink as soon as they were launched.

Graphic Organizer
Directions: Compare the U.S.S. *Monitor* and the C.S.S. *Virginia*. Complete the Venn diagram below.

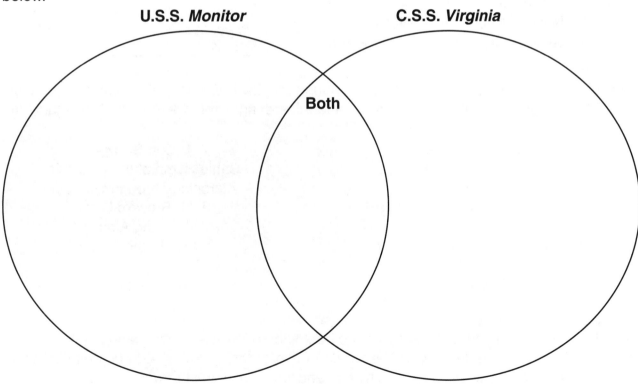

U.S.S. *Monitor*　　　　　　　　　　　　C.S.S. *Virginia*

Both

UNIT TWO: THE CIVIL WAR

Name: _____ Date: _____

Civil War Music

Music was everywhere during the Civil War. Northerners and Southerners each had favorite tunes, many of which are still sung today.

Music played an important role on the Civil War battlefields. Common instruments included bugles, drums, and fifes. These instruments were used to issue marching orders to soldiers.

Music was something soldiers used to lift their spirits while they were marching to a battle. Songs distracted soldiers from the horrors of war, helped them deal with homesickness, and pass the time at night.

Banjos, fiddles, and guitars—occasionally made from cigar boxes—were popular instruments in camp.

One song, "Taps," was originally used to signal the end of the working day in camp. However, during the Civil War, commanders wanted to honor the dead without firing a salute and giving away their position. "Taps" became the song played at military funerals, a practice that continues today. Various lyrics have been written for the song through the years.

Taps
Verse 1: Day is done, gone the sun,
From the lakes, from the hills, from the sky.
All is well, safely rest. God is nigh.

Verse 2: Fading light, dims the sight,
And a star gems the sky, gleaming bright.
From afar, drawing nigh, falls the night.

Verse 3: Thanks and praise, for our days,
'Neath the sun, 'neath the stars, 'neath the sky,
As we go, this we know, God is nigh.

Did You Know?
On three separate occasions, soldiers on both sides of a battlefield had a 'musical duel,' with each side playing their own patriotic songs. In all three occasions, the 'duels' ended with both sides joining together to sing "Home, Sweet Home."

Research
Directions: Many songs that were popular during the Civil War are still played today. Select one of the songs listed below. Learn more about the song. Create a pamphlet to display the information.

Confederate Songs	Union Songs
The Bonnie Blue Flag	Battle Hymn of the Republic
Dixie	Marching Through Georgia
The Yellow Rose of Texas	John Brown's Body
Stonewall Jackson's Way	Marching Along
When Johnny Comes Marching Home Again	Tramp! Tramp! Tramp!
Maryland, My Maryland	The Battle Cry of Freedom
Goober Peas	Give Us a Flag

Step 1: Fold a sheet of white paper in half vertically.
Step 2: Write the name of the song on the front flap and create an illustration
Step 3: On the inside flaps, write the words of two or three verses. Add information about when and why the song was written and what you think the words mean.

Name: _____ Date: _____

Lincoln Issues the Emancipation Proclamation

On January 1, 1863, as Lincoln was about to sign the Emancipation Proclamation, he told the men gathered in his office: "Gentlemen, I never, in my life, felt more certain that I was doing right than in signing this paper."

The Emancipation Proclamation freed slaves in all states or parts of states in rebellion against the United States—about one million slaves.

The new law didn't apply to the three million slaves in states that had not seceded from the Union, or even in certain areas of states that had seceded. The states that had formed the Confederacy ignored the order. Millions of slaves remained slaves.

Lincoln stated his views on slavery very clearly during his presidential campaign. "I will not abolish slavery where it already exists, but we must not let the practice spread. I am opposed to allowing slavery in the new territories."

Lincoln knew that most slave owners would not willingly free their slaves. He did not want to encourage slaves to revolt or use violence if it could be avoided.

The Emancipation Proclamation stated that the government, army, and navy would recognize and maintain the freedom of slaves and would do nothing to stop them from any efforts "they may make for their actual freedom."

"... I hereby enjoin upon the people so declared to be free to abstain from all violence, unless in necessary self-defence; and I recommend to them that, in all cases when allowed, they labor faithfully for reasonable wages," said Lincoln.

Think About It

Why do you think Lincoln issued the Emancipation Proclamation?

Research

Directions: Learn more about the Constitution. Use your research to answer the questions below.

1. Which amendment to the Constitution gave black men the right to vote? _____

2. When was that amendment passed? _____

3. Which amendment to the Constitution gave women the right to vote? _____

4. When was that amendment passed? _____

Black Soldiers Help Win the War

Black soldiers had fought in the Revolutionary War and in the War of 1812, but when they first volunteered to fight in the Civil War, they were refused. Although abolitionists urged President Lincoln to accept blacks as soldiers, the majority of politicians opposed the idea. They believed blacks could not learn the duties and become good soldiers

Frederick Douglass, an escaped slave, questioned this decision. "Why does the government reject the Negro? Is he not a man? Can he not wield a sword, fire a gun, march and countermarch, and obey orders like any other?"

Finally, after two years of war, Congress passed the **Militia Act of 1862**, allowing Lincoln to employ blacks "for any military or naval service for which they may be found competent."

The first black Union regiment, the **54th Massachusetts Volunteers**, received only $10 a month as salary, $3 less than white soldiers. Blacks were not permitted to hold a rank higher than captain.

Union regiments of black soldiers in the South consisted mostly of former slaves, men who knew the territory and had strong motives to fight against their former masters for the freedom of their fellow slaves.

At first, blacks were assigned only to menial tasks like cleaning latrines and building roads. Before the war ended, more than 186,000 blacks had fought in the Union Army and participated in over 400 battles.

Company E, 4th United States Colored Infantry. This detachment was assigned to guard the nation's capital during the Civil War.

Although some white soldiers welcomed the addition of black troops, many objected strongly. Some officers refused to lead black troops; some white soldiers refused to fight alongside them.

In spite of their bravery and outstanding record, **discrimination** against black soldiers continued for nearly another 100 years. It wasn't until 1948 that the army ended **segregation**, and black and white soldiers worked side by side.

Faced with a critical shortage of manpower, Jefferson Davis signed the **Negro Soldier Law** on March 13, 1865. Units of black soldiers were organized in Richmond. Southern crowds threw mud and stones at the soldiers as they trained. However, the war ended soon after, and the Confederate black soldiers never fought in the Civil War.

Name: _____ Date: _____

Black Soldiers Help Win the War (cont.)

Directions: Complete the following exercises.

Matching

_____ 1. Militia Act of 1862

_____ 2. 54th Massachusetts Volunteers

_____ 3. discrimination

_____ 4. segregation

_____ 5. Negro Soldier Law

a. separation

b. signed by Jefferson Davis

c. first black Union regiment

d. prejudice

e. allowed Lincoln to employ blacks "for any military or naval service"

Fill in the Blanks

1. Black soldiers had fought in the _____ _____ and in the War of 1812.

2. Blacks were not permitted to hold a rank higher than _____.

3. Union regiments of black soldiers in the South consisted mostly of former slaves, men who knew the _____ and had strong _____ to fight against their former masters for the freedom of their fellow slaves.

4. Before the war ended, more than _____ blacks had fought in the Union Army and participated in over _____ battles.

5. However, the war ended soon after, and the _____ black soldiers never fought in the Civil War.

True or False

Directions: Write "T" if the statement is true or "F" if it is false.

1. T F Abolitionists opposed the idea of blacks as soldiers.

2. T F Black soldiers did not fight in the Revolutionary War.

3. T F Politicians urged President Lincoln to accept blacks as soldiers.

4. T F Frederick Douglass was an escaped slave.

5. T F The 54th Massachusetts Volunteers received only $10 a month in salary.

6. T F Discrimination against black soldiers continued for nearly another 100 years after the Civil War.

7. T F It wasn't until 1998 that the army ended segregation, and black and white soldiers worked side by side.

8. T F Faced with a critical shortage of manpower, Jefferson Davis signed the Negro Soldier Law on March 13, 1865.

9. T F Confederate black soldiers never fought in the Civil War.

10. T F Union regiments of black soldiers in South Carolina consisted mostly of former slaves.

Name: _____ Date: _____

Women and the Civil War

When the Civil War began, women were not allowed to vote. They had no say in politics and could not join the army. All the leaders in both the North and South were white men who believed women should not have paying jobs and were capable only of taking care of their homes and children.

Even though they were officially excluded, it didn't mean women did not participate. When husbands, fathers, and sons joined the army, wives, sisters, and mothers were left to run the homes, businesses, farms, and plantations. They plowed fields and planted and harvested crops.

Male teachers joined the army; women kept the schools running. When there was a shortage of male factory workers in the North, women learned to fill those jobs too.

Dorothea Dix, who reformed prisons and hospitals, was put in charge of recruiting and training nurses. Clara Barton, founder of the American Red Cross, and Louisa May Alcott, a famous writer, were among the many women who worked as nurses during the Civil War.

Women cared for injured and sick soldiers, kept the hospitals as clean as possible, and ran convalescent homes. They raised money through bake sales and carnivals to

Clara Barton, founder of the American Red Cross

buy supplies for troops. They knitted socks and made clothing for the soldiers.

Some women became spies. Pauline Cushman, an actress, traveled to the South and returned with information for the Union Army. Harriet Tubman served the Union Army as a cook, spy, nurse, and scout, but she was never paid for her work.

During the four long years of the Civil War, women learned new skills and found they could be self-reliant. Yet when the men returned from the war, they expected women to quietly accept their former subservient roles. More and more women came to believe they were entitled to equal rights.

Critical Thinking

How do you think women felt when they were expected to return to their former roles after the war, when many had worked a full-time job in addition to taking care of a home and children for several years during the war?

_____

_____

_____

_____

Lincoln's Gettysburg Address

Early on the morning of July 1, 1863, the Battle at Gettysburg began. The fighting lasted for three terrible days. When the armies left the battlefield, dead horses, broken muskets, and bayonets were scattered across the area. Barns and farmhouses were destroyed, livestock was dead, and wheat and cornfields were ruined.

Much, much worse were the thousands of shallow graves of those who died in the bloodiest battle of the Civil War. Over 50,000 Union and Confederate soldiers died or were injured. The dead were buried on the battlefield.

President Lincoln was invited to speak at the dedication of a cemetery in Gettysburg, Pennsylvania, on November 19, 1863. Lincoln's speech lasted less than two minutes, but it has become the best-remembered speech in American history.

Lincoln's Gettysburg Address

Fourscore and seven years ago our fathers brought forth on this continent a new nation, **conceived** in liberty and dedicated to the proposition that all men are created equal.

Now we are engaged in a great civil war, testing whether that nation or any nation so conceived and so dedicated can long endure. We are met on a great battlefield of that war. We have come to dedicate a portion of that field, as a final resting-place for those who here gave their lives that that nation might live. It is altogether fitting and proper that we should do this.

But, in a larger sense, we can not dedicate—we can not **consecrate**—we can not **hallow**—this ground. The brave men, living and dead, who struggled here, have consecrated it, far above our poor power to add or detract. The world will little note, nor long remember, what we say here, but it can never forget what they did here. It is for us the living, rather, to be dedicated here to the unfinished work which they who fought here have thus far so nobly advanced. It is rather for us to be here dedicated to the great task remaining before us—that from these honored dead we take increased devotion to that cause for which they gave the last full measure of devotion—that we here highly resolve that these dead shall not have died in vain—that this nation, under God, shall have a new birth of freedom—and that government of the people, by the people, for the people, shall not perish from the earth.

Name: _____ Date: _____

Lincoln's Gettysburg Address (cont.)

Directions: Complete the following exercises.

Matching

_____ 1. conceived

_____ 2. consecrate

_____ 3. hallow

_____ 4. Gettysburg Address

_____ 5. Four score and seven years

a. to make sacred

b. speech Lincoln gave at the ceremony dedicating the cemetery to soldiers who had died in the Battle of Gettysburg

c. 87 years

d. to set apart as holy

e. created

Constructed Response

1. What was Lincoln's purpose for giving the speech? Give specific details or examples to support your answer.

_____

_____

_____

2. What tasks does Lincoln say must still be done? Give specific details or examples to support your answer.

_____

_____

_____

Critical Thinking

Why do you think the Gettysburg Address has become one of the best-remembered speeches in American history?

_____

_____

_____

_____

Activity

Directions: Study the copy of the Gettysburg Address on page 68. Present your own dramatic interpretation of the Gettysburg Address, demonstrating the public-speaking skills necessary to communicate effectively with an audience, such as voice level, tone, and inflection.

The Civil War Ends

Following a ten-month siege of **Richmond, Virginia**, the capital of the Confederacy, **General Robert E. Lee** ordered his troops to retreat. Union troops took Richmond and continued a running battle with the rear guard of the retreating troops.

General Ulysses S. Grant realized that if he continued to push his advantage, there was a good chance that General Lee would surrender. President Lincoln agreed and gave the order to proceed.

For six days, Lee's men continued to fight as they fled west. Out of supplies, the army arrived at the small village of **Appomattox Court House, Virginia**.

General Grant sent a message under a flag of truce offering to accept Lee's surrender. On April 9, 1865, General Robert E. Lee agreed. Grant ordered an immediate cease-fire.

When they met in the front parlor of a two-story brick farmhouse, General Lee surrendered all men, arms, ammunition, and supplies except the horses and mules that were the personal property of the soldiers.

General Lee also offered to return about 1,000 Union soldiers who were prisoners of war because he had no food for them. Grant accepted his offer and then sent beef, bread, coffee, and sugar to feed the Confederate troops.

When Union soldiers began firing cannon salutes to celebrate the end of the war, General Grant ordered all loud celebrations ended. "The war is over, the rebels are our countrymen again," he told them.

More than 620,000 Americans died in the Civil War. Thousands more were wounded or seriously ill. Over one-fifth of the adult white males in the South died. Men returned to their families blind, deaf, or missing arms and legs. 37,000 African-Americans died fighting for their freedom.

Lincoln looked forward to "a just and lasting peace." His goal was to help both sides recover and rebuild. At his first public appearance after the war, Lincoln asked the band to play "**Dixie**," a favorite Southern song. "I have always thought 'Dixie' one of the best tunes I have ever heard," he said.

UNIT TWO: THE CIVIL WAR

Name: _____ Date: _____

The Civil War Ends (cont.)

Matching

_____ 1. General Robert E. Lee

_____ 2. Appomattox Court House, Virginia

_____ 3. "Dixie"

_____ 4. Richmond, Virginia

_____ 5. General Ulysses S. Grant

a. Union general

b. small village where the Confederate army surrendered to the Union army

c. Confederate general

d. capital of the Confederacy

e. Southern song

Fill in the Blanks

1. More than 600,000 _____ died in the Civil War.

2. Over _____ of the adult white males in the South died.

3. 37,000 _____-_____ died fighting for their freedom.

4. Lincoln looked forward to "a just and lasting peace." His goal was to help both sides _____ and _____.

5. At his first public appearance after the war, Lincoln asked the band to play "Dixie," a favorite _____ song.

Constructed Response

Describe the terms General Lee agreed to in the surrender. Give specific details or examples.

_____

_____

_____

_____

_____

Critical Thinking

Describe how you think Lincoln felt when he learned that General Lee had surrendered. Give specific details or examples to support your opinion.

_____

_____

_____

_____

_____

_____

The Assassination of Lincoln

On April 14, 1865, the Lincolns and their guests arrived at **Ford's Theatre** after the play had started. Lincoln's bodyguard, John Parker, left his post outside the door of the president's box so he could watch the play. Some time later, he left the theater.

John Wilkes Booth rode to the theater on a rented horse. He asked one of the stage-hands to hold his horse while he went into the theater. Surprised not to find a guard at the door to the passage leading to the president's box, he blocked the door from the inside with a piece of wood he had hidden earlier and then watched the president.

As the audience laughed at the lines spoken by one of the actors, Booth stepped up behind the president, aimed, and pulled the trigger. The bullet entered Lincoln's head.

Henry Rathbone, Lincoln's guest at the play, struggled with Booth. Booth pulled a knife, slashed Rathbone, and jumped over the railing to the stage. He fell awkwardly, breaking his left ankle. On stage, Booth shouted the Latin motto of Virginia, "**Sic Semper Tyrannis**," which means "Thus always with tyrants."

The Assassination of President Lincoln
by Currier and Ives

Limping away, Booth leaped on his horse and galloped off. Screams filled the theater. Rathbone had to remove the wood blocking the door before anyone could enter.

The first doctor to arrive was **Charles Leale**, a young army surgeon. By then the president was unconscious and barely breathing. After examining him, Leale told the others, "His wound is mortal. It is impossible for him to recover."

Carefully, the president was carried across the street to **Peterson's Boarding-house**. Doctors made two unsuccessful attempts to remove the bullet. Lincoln never regained consciousness. He died the following morning at 7:22 A.M.

Did You Know?

Eleven years after Lincoln died, grave robbers broke into his tomb. They dragged the casket partially out before being caught and arrested. Since there was no law against body snatching at the time, they were charged with breaking and entering. They served a year in prison.

UNIT TWO: THE CIVIL WAR

Name: _____ Date: _____

The Assassination of Lincoln (cont.)

Directions: Complete the following exercises.

Matching

_____ 1. Ford's Theatre

_____ 2. John Wilkes Booth

_____ 3. Peterson's Boardinghouse

_____ 4. Charles Leale

_____ 5. "Sic Semper Tyrannis"

a. place where Lincoln was shot by an assassin

b. "Thus always with tyrants"

c. where Lincoln was cared for until his death

d. first doctor to arrive after Lincoln was shot

e. actor who shot Lincoln

Fill in the Blanks

1. Lincoln's bodyguard, _____ _____, left his post outside the door of the president's box so he could watch the play.

2. John Wilkes Booth rode to the theater on a rented _____.

3. As the audience laughed at the lines spoken by one of the actors, _____ stepped up behind the president, aimed, and pulled the trigger.

4. _____ _____, Lincoln's guest at the play, struggled with Booth.

5. Lincoln never regained _____. He _____ the following morning at 7:22 A.M.

Critical Thinking

Lincoln's bodyguard left his post the night Lincoln was shot. How might things have been different if he had stayed outside the president's box? Give specific details or examples to support your opinion.

_____

_____

_____

_____

_____

Technology in the Classroom
Primary Source: <http://digital.library.mcgill.ca/lincoln/exhibit/>
("Taft Journal." McGill University)

Directions: On April 14, 1865, President Lincoln was shot by John Wilkes Booth. He was carried unconscious to a neighboring house, where Dr. C. S. Taft attended to him. Dr. Taft kept a detailed record of Lincoln's injuries and care until his death. Read Dr. Taft's journal. Research the events surrounding the assassination and death of Lincoln. From the perspective of an eyewitness, write journal entries about the events surrounding the assassination.

Name: _____ Date: _____

The Rest of the Story

After John Wilkes Booth escaped from Ford's Theatre, he met David Herold. They rode to a tavern owned by Mary Surratt, mother of another of the **conspirators**, where they had met on several occasions to discuss their plans. They retrieved a rifle and went on to the home of Dr. Mudd, a Southern sympathizer Booth knew. Dr. Mudd set Booth's broken ankle and let Booth and Herold spend the night.

The following afternoon, Booth and Herold rode to the home of another Southern sympathizer. Samuel Cox and his foster brother Thomas Jones knew who Booth was and what he had done. Jones hid the men in a grove of pine trees for six days and supplied them with food and newspapers.

Authorities arrested the other conspirators except for John Surratt, who fled to Canada, then Europe. Mary Surratt, Dr. Mudd, and the stagehand who held Booth's horse were also taken into custody. The government offered a reward of $100,000 for Booth's capture.

Booth and Herold fled south. Federal authorities caught up with them in a storage shed near Port Royal, Virginia. Herold surrendered; Booth refused. The shed was set on fire; Booth was shot and killed. The surviving conspirators were tried and found guilty. Herold, George Atzerodt, Lewis Powell, and Mary

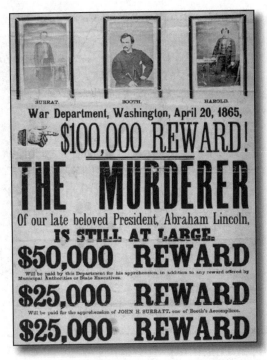

Surratt were hanged on July 7, 1865. Dr. Mudd, Samuel Arnold, and Michael O'Laughlen were sentenced to life in prison. Even the stagehand who had held Booth's horse was sentenced to six years in prison.

Although Booth killed Lincoln, his plan to throw the government into chaos failed. People in the North blamed the entire South for the actions of John Wilkes Booth, making it even more difficult to mend the hard feelings caused by the Civil War.

Graphic Organizer

Directions: Complete the vocabulary chart by creating a definition, using the word in a sentence, and drawing an illustration that helps you remember the meaning of the word.

Word	Definition	Illustration
conspirators		
	Sentence	

Name: _____ Date: _____

After the War

When the Civil War was finally over, more than 620,000 Americans had died. Thousands more had been wounded or were seriously ill. Men returned to their families blind, deaf, or missing arms and legs.

Families lost sons, fathers, brothers, and husbands. Over one-fifth of the adult white males in the South had died. Another 37,000 African-Americans had died fighting for their freedom.

Families were split apart. Brothers had fought each other. In some families, the bitter feelings caused by the war never healed.

Kentucky's Senator John Crittenden had had two sons who were generals in the Civil War: one serving in the Confederate Army, the other in the Union Army.

Property damage was so extensive in the South that some areas took years to recover. Farmland was ruined and farm animals had been killed. Cities were in ruins; homes had been burned, crops destroyed, and railroad lines torn up. Confederate money was worthless.

The slaves were free, but free to do what? Most had no land, no homes, no education, no money, and no skills.

Critical Thinking

Directions: Give specific details or examples to support your opinion.

1. Imagine being a woman with four children. Your home was burned down during the war. All your farm animals were killed. When your husband returns, he is an invalid and cannot do any kind of work. What can you do to pick up the pieces and start a new life?

   _____

   _____

   _____

   _____

   _____

2. Imagine being a former male slave in the South. You are free at last but have nowhere to go, no home, no money, and no skills other than working in a cotton field. You have a wife and two children living with you. Your other two children were sold to a different master, and you have no idea where they are. How do you feel about your freedom?

   _____

   _____

   _____

   _____

   _____

Name: _____ Date: _____

Research

Directions: Learn more about one of the topics listed below. Construct a pyramid to display your research.

People

Mary Todd Lincoln	Stephen Douglas	Jefferson Davis	Hannibal Hamlin
Andrew Johnson	John Wilkes Booth	George Atzerodt	David Herold
Lewis Powell	Ulysses S. Grant	Robert E. Lee	

Places

Ford's Theatre

Appomattox Court House

Other

Emancipation Proclamation   13th Amendment

Gettysburg Address   Battle at Gettysburg

1. Fold a white sheet of paper from the top of the right corner to the left hand edge of the paper as shown below. Cut off the leftover piece at the bottom. You will have a triangle left.

2. Fold your triangle in half and then unfold the paper.

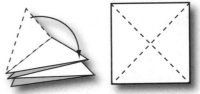

3. Cut one fold to the center of the triangle.

4. Place an x on one of the flaps. Write your title on the other flap. Write your research information on the two triangles.

5. Put glue on the flap with an x. Fold the title flap over the x flap and glue together.

Civil War Battles Research

The Civil War was a costly and lengthy one for both the Union and the Confederacy. Beginning with the battle at Fort Sumter on April 12, 1861, the war continued until General Robert E. Lee surrendered at Appomattox Court House on April 9, 1865. Even after that, there were battles in other parts of the South until all the Southern armies surrendered.

Both sides achieved many victories and suffered many defeats. Battles were fought on land and at sea; as far north as Gettysburg, Pennsylvania, and as far south as Florida and New Orleans.

Directions: Learn more about one of the Civil War battles listed below. On your own paper, write a newspaper article about the battle. In your article, answer these questions:

- Who commanded the Union Army in that battle?
- Who commanded the Confederate Army in that battle?
- When and where was this battle fought? Who won it?
- Why was this battle fought, and why was it important?
- What did both sides hope to accomplish?
- How did this battle affect the outcome of the Civil War?

Some battles fought during the Civil War were:

Antietam	Gettysburg
Atlanta	Holly Springs
Baton Rouge	Huntsville
Bent Creek	Kennesaw Mountain
Brandy Station	Mechanicsville
Bull Run	Milliken's Bend
Chancellorsville	Missionary Ridge
Chattanooga	Murfreesboro
Chickamauga	Nashville
Chicksaw Bluffs	New Orleans
Cold Harbor	Pea Ridge
Corinth	Shiloh
Fort Donelson	Spotsylvania
Fort Henry	Vicksburg
Fort Sumter	The Wilderness
Fredericksburg	

UNIT TWO: THE CIVIL WAR

Name: _____ Date: _____

The Reconstruction Era Time Line

1865 **March 3:** Congress established the Freedmen's Bureau.
March 4: Lincoln began his second term as president.
April 9: The Civil War ended when General Lee surrendered.
April 14: Lincoln was assassinated by John Wilkes Booth.
April 15: Andrew Johnson became president.
December 18: The Thirteenth Amendment abolished slavery.

1866 **February 19:** The new Freedmen's Bureau Bill was passed.
April 9: The Civil Rights Act was passed.
May 1: The Memphis race riot occurred.
July 30: The New Orleans race riot occurred.

1867 **January 8:** Black citizens in Washington, D.C., were granted the right to vote.
March 1: Nebraska became a state.
March 2: The first Reconstruction Act was passed.
March 2: The Tenure of Office Act was passed.
April: Alaska was purchased from Russia for $7.2 million in gold.

1868 Arkansas, Alabama, Florida, Louisiana, and North and South Carolina were readmitted
to the Union.
February 24: Congress voted to impeach Andrew Johnson.
March 23: President Johnson's impeachment trial began.
May 16: President Johnson was acquitted.
July 28: The Fourteenth Amendment was passed.
November 3: Ulysses S. Grant was elected president.
December 25: Unconditional amnesty was granted by presidential proclamation to all
participants in the "insurrection or rebellion" against the United States.

1870 Georgia, Mississippi, Texas, and Virginia were readmitted as states.
February 25: The first black U.S. senator entered Congress.
March 30: The Fifteenth Amendment was passed.
June 27: Congress established the Department of Justice.

1871 **February 28:** The Federal Election Law was passed.

1872 **November 5:** President Grant was reelected.

1875 **March 1:** The Civil Rights Act granted blacks equal rights in public places and allowed
them to serve on juries.

1876 **December 6:** Rutherford B. Hayes was elected president by the vote of an electoral commission set up by Congress after electoral votes in three states were in dispute.

1877 **June 15:** Henry O. Fipper became the first African American to graduate from the U.S.
Military Academy at West Point.

Name: _____ Date: _____

Reconstruction Time Line Activity

Directions: Number the events in order from 1 (first) to 20 (last). Use the time line for reference.

_____ A. Ulysses S. Grant became president.

_____ B. Rutherford B. Hayes became president.

_____ C. Andrew Johnson became president.

_____ D. Congress passed the first Civil Rights Act.

_____ E. Congress established the Freedmen's Bureau.

_____ F. Arkansas, Alabama, Florida, Louisiana, and North and South Carolina were readmitted as states.

_____ G. The United States purchased Alaska from Russia.

_____ H. The Fourteenth Amendment passed.

_____ I. The amendment abolishing slavery was passed.

_____ J. Georgia, Mississippi, Texas, and Virginia were readmitted as states.

_____ K. Congress voted to impeach President Johnson.

_____ L. Congress passed the first Reconstruction Act.

_____ M. Blacks were granted equal rights in public places.

_____ N. The Federal Election Law was passed.

_____ O. The New Orleans race riot occurred.

_____ P. Henry O. Fipper became the first African American to graduate from West Point.

_____ Q. Congress established the Department of Justice.

_____ R. The Fifteenth Amendment was passed.

_____ S. President Johnson was acquitted.

_____ T. The first black U.S. Senator entered Congress.

Reconstruction

When the Civil War was finally over, 620,000 Americans had died. Thousands more had been wounded or were seriously ill. Men returned to their families blind, deaf, or missing arms and legs.

Families lost sons, fathers, brothers, and husbands. Over 250,000 Confederate soldiers had been killed. Another 37,000 African-Americans had died fighting for their freedom.

Families were split apart. Brothers had fought each other. In some families, the bitter feelings caused by the war never healed.

Kentucky's Senator John Crittenden had had two sons who were generals in the Civil War: one serving in the **Confederate Army**, the other in the **Union Army**.

The South was in shambles. Property damage was so extensive in the South that some areas took years to recover. The Union Army had destroyed homes, businesses, farm animals, and fields. Cities were in ruins; homes had been burned, crops destroyed, and railroad lines torn up.

The Southern economy was ruined. Confederate money was worthless. The social system that had existed in the South before the Civil War had been destroyed.

The slaves were free, but free to do what? Most had no land, no homes, no education, no money, and no skills.

With the Confederate government powerless, the North clearly had to deal with

The Atlanta, Georgia, railroad roundhouse is shown in ruins, shortly after the Civil War ended.

the situation. The plan for rebuilding the South and reuniting it with the Union was known as **Reconstruction** (1865–1877).

Most Northerners believed that Reconstruction was necessary because of conditions in the Southern states, but few agreed on what should be done. They also disagreed about how to ensure the freedom and civil rights of former slaves.

Reconstruction caused one of the greatest disputes in the United States. People today still argue about it.

Even though there were many different ideas about how Reconstruction should be handled, most of the debates involved two opposing viewpoints: the **radical** approach favored by Congress and the **moderate** approach proposed by President Abraham Lincoln.

Reconstruction (cont.)

Directions: Complete the following exercises.

Matching

_____ 1. Union Army

_____ 2. Confederate Army

_____ 3. Reconstruction

_____ 4. radical

_____ 5. moderate

a. extreme

b. rebuilding of the South after the end of the Civil War

c. army of the North

d. army of the South

e. neither extreme nor conservative

Fill in the Blanks

1. Over 250,000 _____ soldiers had been killed.

2. Property damage was so extensive in the _____ that some areas took years to recover.

3. The _____ _____ that had existed in the South before the Civil War had been destroyed.

4. Most Northerners believed that _____ was necessary because of conditions in the Southern states, but few agreed on what should be done.

5. Reconstruction caused one of the greatest _____ in the United States.

Critical Thinking

Congress felt that the South should pay a high price for its disloyalty. Give specific details or examples to support your opinion.

_____

_____

_____

_____

_____

_____

_____

_____

_____

_____

_____

_____

Name: _____ Date: _____

Lincoln's Ten Percent Plan

The Civil War began with the Battle at Fort Sumter in 1861. Eleven states broke away from the Union and formed their own country, the Confederate States of America.

The Civil War continued much longer than anyone expected. It did not end until General Lee surrendered to General Grant on April 9, 1865. Several battles were fought even after that in other parts of the South until all the Southern armies surrendered.

Even before the Civil War ended, however, people talked about what would happen when the country was again at peace. How would the Confederate States be reunited with the United States? What penalties should be imposed on the people of the states that had seceded?

President Lincoln had a simple plan for reuniting the nation. Known as the "Ten Percent Plan," it required that ten percent of the voters in a state that had joined the Confederacy must take an oath of loyalty to the United States. Then the state could send representatives to Congress, and the state would be readmitted to the Union.

Northerners who supported Lincoln's plan were called moderates. They, like Lincoln, believed that the Southern states should not be harshly punished for seceding from the Union and should be readmitted as quickly as possible.

Lincoln looked forward to "a just and lasting peace." His goal was to help both sides recover and rebuild. At his first public appearance after the war, Lincoln asked the band to play "Dixie," a favorite Southern song. "I have always thought 'Dixie' one of the best tunes I have ever heard," he said.

Unfortunately, Lincoln was assassinated before he could implement his plan.

Critical Thinking

Why do you think Abraham Lincoln asked the band to play "Dixie" at his first public appearance after the war? Give specific details or examples to support your answer.

_____

_____

_____

_____

_____

_____

_____

Name: _____ Date: _____

The Thirteenth Amendment

When Abraham Lincoln issued the **Emancipation** Proclamation on January 1, 1863, he freed slaves in all states or parts of states in rebellion against the United States—about one million slaves.

Howev-er, this did not include free-dom for the three million slaves in states that had not se-ceded from the Union or even in certain areas of states that had seceded.

In De-cember 1865, the Thirteenth Amendment to the Constitution of the United States finally freed all slaves within the United

States and made slavery illegal forever. It also gave Congress the power to enforce this amendment.

Amendment 13

Section 1. Neither slavery nor involuntary servitude, except as punishment for crime whereof the party shall have been duly convicted, shall exist within the United States, or any place sub-ject to their jurisdiction.

However, Southern blacks now faced the difficulty Northern blacks had confront-ed—that of freedmen surrounded by hostile whites.

One freedman, Houston Hartsfield Hol-loway, wrote, "For we colored people did not know how to be free, and the white people did not know how to have a free colored person about them."

Graphic Organizer

Directions: Complete the vocabulary chart by creating a definition, using the word in a sentence, and drawing an illustration that helps you remember the meaning of the word.

Word	Definition	Illustration
emancipation		
	Sentence	

Name: _____ Date: _____

Andrew Johnson

Andrew Johnson was only three years old when his father died. His mother worked hard to support her two sons, but there was never enough money. School cost money and was out of the question. "If being poor was a crime," Johnson once said, "I should have to plead that I was guilty."

In 1822, Johnson's mother arranged for 13-year-old Andrew and his brother to become apprentice tailors. In exchange for food and clothing, he and his brother worked for the tailor and learned the trade.

Andrew's family was one of many who journeyed west to start over. They settled in Greeneville, Tennessee. Andrew got a job as a tailor and met Eliza McCardle. They were married in 1827. Although he could read a little, he didn't know how to write his own name.

Johnson opened his own tailor shop. While he worked, his wife read to him. In the evenings, she taught him to write and do simple arithmetic.

He won his first election at the age of 19 when he was elected village alderman of Greeneville, Tennessee. Two years later, he was elected village mayor.

In 1835, Johnson won election to the state legislature. Johnson voted against what he considered wasteful government spending. He refused to approve money to improve state roads and funds for a railroad. Those two decisions cost him the next election.

By moderating his views on "internal improvements," he was reelected several more times to the state legislature and then to the U.S. House of Representatives in 1843.

Often Johnson upheld the views of most Southerners, including the belief that slavery was necessary for the Southern economy. However, he was not afraid to side with the North or even take an independent view when he believed he was right. His refusal to always side with one side or the other earned him both praise and political enemies.

After serving ten years in the House, Johnson lost his bid for the Senate. However, he ran for and was elected governor of Tennessee in 1853.

Critical Thinking

Do you think it likely that a person who was 19 and had almost no education could be elected to any office today? Why or why not? Give specific details or examples to support your answer.

_____

_____

_____

_____

_____

_____

_____

Name: _____ Date: _____

Andrew Johnson Becomes President

Andrew Johnson

Throughout Johnson's political career, his popularity was with the common men of the state. His wealthy political opponents ridiculed his humble origins and lack of formal education.

"Some day I will show the stuck-up aristocrats who is running the country," Johnson once said. "They are … not as good as the man who earns his bread by the sweat of his brow."

As governor of Tennessee, Johnson es-

tablished the state's first public school system and founded the state's first public library.

After two terms as governor, Johnson was elected to the U.S. Senate. When the Southern states formed the Confederacy, Johnson was the only Southern senator who refused to give up his seat in Congress. Johnson blamed the Civil War and secession on wealthy white plantation owners.

"I shall stay inside the Union and there fight for Southern rights. I advise all others to do the same."

Many Northerners applauded Johnson for supporting the Union. When Lincoln ran for his second term of office in 1864, he invited Johnson to be his running mate.

After Lincoln was assassinated, Andrew Johnson became president.

Did You Know?
The plot to assassinate Abraham Lincoln also included a plan to kill Vice President Johnson and other top government officials.

Critical Thinking
Considering Johnson's lack of formal education, why do you think his efforts to establish a public school system and public libraries were important to him? Give specific details or examples to support your answer.

_____

_____

_____

_____

_____

_____

Name: _____ Date: _____

Reconstruction Under President Johnson

Shortly after Johnson became president, Congress recessed for the summer. Northern Radicals expected Johnson to continue to support their plans for Reconstruction. However, Johnson did not favor equal rights for blacks. He believed that "White men alone must manage the South." Johnson offered blacks no role in Reconstruction.

Johnson's plan for Reconstruction was even more liberal than Lincoln's. He required only that the Southern states agree that slavery and secession were illegal.

Once that was done, they were allowed to elect their own leaders and members of Congress. Johnson believed only whites should be allowed to vote. He encouraged the Southern states to rejoin the Union as quickly as possible.

Since freedmen were not allowed to vote, many former Confederate leaders, including the former Confederate vice president, were elected to high positions in the South and in Congress.

In the summer of 1865, Johnson pardoned hundreds of former Rebel soldiers. His pardon was automatic except for those who were wealthy. Having grown up poor, Johnson always resented those who had money.

Anyone with assets of $20,000 or more had to apply in person to receive a pardon. By the summer of 1866, Johnson had pardoned almost everyone.

With the former leaders of the Southern states back in control, the states passed laws known as the Black Codes, which were designed to keep former slaves in conditions very close to slavery. Violence and racism were common.

When Congress went into session in December 1865, those who had hoped for a peaceful and quick Reconstruction were alarmed by Johnson's policies. Northern members refused to allow Southerners to participate in Congress until their states had been readmitted to the Union. They criticized the way Johnson had handled Reconstruction.

Johnson demanded the recognition of congressmen from the South and declared that Reconstruction was finished.

Think About It

President Andrew Johnson offered a reward of $100,000 for the capture of Jefferson Davis. In today's dollars, that would be the equivalent of over one million dollars.

Constructed Response

What was President Johnson's opinion or view of the role of blacks in Reconstruction? Give specific details to support your answer.

_____

_____

_____

_____

UNIT THREE: RECONSTRUCTION

Name: _____ Date: _____

The Black Codes of 1865 and 1866

After the Civil War, newly freed slaves soon learned that freedom was not what they expected it to be. Many of the former Confederate states passed laws known as the Black Codes. These laws were based on the slave codes that had been in effect since early colonial days.

The Black Codes were intended to keep the social situation in the South as close as possible to what it had been before the Civil War. Even though slaves were legally free, they were allowed very little freedom.

The Black Codes were designed to continue providing cheap sources of labor for White Southerners and were based on the belief that blacks were inferior beings. Blacks were required to sign yearly labor contracts, often with their former masters.

Blacks who were unemployed and without a permanent residence could be declared vagrants. Vagrants were arrested and fined. If unable to pay, they were forced to work to pay off the fine.

Some states limited the types of property freedmen could own and where they could live. They were excluded from certain businesses or from specific trades in some states.

Former slaves were not allowed to carry firearms, meet in unsupervised groups, or testify in court against whites. Freedmen could not vote or hold public office. They had to receive permission to travel and were forbidden to live in many cities. They were allowed to marry, but interracial marriage was strictly forbidden.

The harsh Black Codes and treatment of freedmen by Southern whites were part of the reason Congress took such a radical view of Reconstruction. The situation in the South prompted the passage of the Fourteenth and Fifteenth Amendments to the Constitution.

Reconstruction eliminated the Black Codes, but many of the restrictions of the Black Codes became legal again under a series of Jim Crow laws. Some of these laws were not abolished until passage of the Civil Rights Act of 1964.

Constructed Response

What are vagrants? Give specific details or examples to support your answer.

_____

_____

_____

_____

_____

_____

Name: _____   Date: _____

Carl Schurz Reports to the President

Carl Schurz

Carl Schurz, a German immigrant, passed his bar exam in Milwaukee, Wisconsin, in 1859. He became a close friend of Abraham Lincoln, who appointed him U.S. Minister to Spain in 1861. After serving in the Union Army during the Civil War, he became a journalist.

After the war, President Andrew Johnson sent Carl Schurz to the South to report on conditions firsthand. He wanted to know how well Reconstruction was working and the actual status of freedmen.

Schurz spent months touring the South, talking to army personnel, Southern leaders, and common people, both black and white.

Everywhere he went, he found similar problems.

Most former slaves were trying to start new lives. They wanted to own homes, hold good jobs, and provide education for themselves and their children.

Schurz found that for the most part, however, the attitudes of Southerners had not changed. In spite of the Emancipation Proclamation and the Thirteenth Amendment, they still viewed blacks as property, not people.

Some plantation owners kept their former slaves nearby, living in the same places, working in the same fields, doing the same jobs they had done when they were slaves.

Schurz reported that blacks were attacked, their schools, churches, and homes burned, and their rights denied.

In spite of Schurz's report, President Johnson continued with his Reconstruction policies.

Constructed Response

From his tour of the South, what did Carl Schurz discover about the attitudes of the groups listed below? Give specific details or examples to support your answer.

Former slaves _____

_____

_____

Southerners _____

_____

_____

Name: _____ Date: _____

The Freedmen's Bureau

After Lincoln issued the Emancipation Proclamation, thousands of former slaves, called freedmen, ran away from their owners. Most had no property, few skills, no education, and nowhere to go.

The U.S. Bureau of Refugees, Freedmen, and Abandoned Lands was established by Congress on March 3, 1865, to provide health care, education, and assistance to freedmen. By the time the Civil War ended, the bureau had opened offices throughout the South and had begun providing relief to both blacks and whites.

Besides providing aid to four million African Americans, the Freedmen's Bureau opened more than 1,000 schools for blacks and spent over $400,000 to establish teacher training centers. It opened hospitals and provided medical assistance to over a million people.

In February 1866, Congress wanted to give the bureau more power to defend freedmen against the Black Codes.

President Johnson vetoed the bill. Johnson declared that states should have the right to make their own laws and the federal government shouldn't interfere. Congress overrode the president's veto and passed the Freedmen's Bill on February 19, 1866.

Although it did much to help Southern blacks, the bureau had inadequate funds and poorly trained personnel. As more and more of the power was drained away from this agency, it eventually did little more than oversee sharecropping arrangements. Congress terminated the bureau in July 1872.

Critical Thinking

Do you agree or disagree with Johnson that states should have the right to make their own laws without federal interference? Why or why not? Give specific details or examples to support your answer.

_____

_____

_____

_____

_____

_____

_____

Name: _____ Date: _____

How Congress Passes Laws

Article I of the U.S. Constitution established the way new laws are introduced and approved.

A proposed law is first introduced as a bill, usually in the House of Representatives. Members of both branches of Congress discuss the bill. At that point it may be rewritten. A majority of members of both the Senate and the House must approve the bill before it is sent to the president for approval.

The president has several choices.

A. If the president approves and signs the bill within ten days, it becomes a law.

B. If the president objects to the bill, he can return it to the house in which it originated within ten days with an explanation of his objections. This is called a **veto**.

   1. Then the House and Senate can either change the bill and resubmit it to the president for approval or take another vote on the original bill.

2. If two-thirds of the members of both the Senate and House of Representatives vote to pass the original bill, it becomes a law even without the president's approval. This is called **overriding a veto**.

C. If the president does not sign the bill within ten days and does not return it to Congress, it automatically becomes a law unless Congress has adjourned.

While he was president, Andrew Johnson vetoed 29 bills; Congress overrode 15 of those vetoes.

Fill in the Blank

1. The _____ established how new laws are made.

2. When Congress feels a new law is needed, a _____ is introduced.

3. A _____ of members of the Senate and House of Representatives must approve the bill before it goes to the president.

4. If the president does not agree to sign a bill, he can return it to Congress within _____ days.

5. Then _____ of the members of both the Senate and House must vote to approve the original bill for it to become a law.

Name: _____ Date: _____

No Homes for the Homeless

In January 1865, General Sherman issued Special Field Order No. 15, setting aside abandoned lands on the sea islands and along the coast of South Carolina and Georgia for exclusive use by freed slaves from the region.

One of the original responsibilities of the Freedmen's Bureau was to help homeless blacks find places to live. Congressman Charles Sumner urged the government to divide up the large Southern plantations and give the land to former slaves.

President Johnson reversed General Sherman's order. As he pardoned Southerners, Johnson returned their lands to them. Even though they didn't agree with the president on most items regarding Reconstruction, Congress refused to consider any form of land redistribution.

General William Tecumsah Sherman

Cause and Effect

Directions: A **cause** is an event that produces a result. An **effect** is the result produced. For each statement below, write a cause or effect.

1. **Cause:** _____

_____

Effect: Set aside abandoned lands on the sea islands and along the coast of South Carolina and Georgia for exclusive use by freed slaves from the region.

2. **Cause:** Freedmen's Bureau

Effect: _____

_____

3. **Cause:** President Johnson reversed Special Field Order No. 15.

Effect: _____

_____

Southern Congressmen Turned Away

Congress did not meet for regular sessions between May and December 1865. During that time, President Johnson had a free hand to **implement** his Reconstruction policies. He quickly readmitted all the former Confederate states except Texas to the Union.

When Congress met in December, they were amazed and outraged to find that the South had elected men who had led the fight against the Union only six months earlier as new members to Congress.

The number of members a state has in the U.S. House of Representatives is based on population. Previously, blacks had only been counted as three-fifths of a person. Now that they were freed, each black person was counted as a whole person. That change meant that the South would have at least 12 more representatives in Congress.

As a result, the Northern Republicans would no longer be able to control policies regarding the South, and the Southerners were back in Congress, stronger than ever.

Although it was dishonest and unfair, **Radical Republicans** disqualified the Southern congressmen; then they appointed a committee to study the matter. Of course, the committee consisted only of Radical Republicans.

Led by **Thaddeus Stevens**, this group became known as the **Committee of Fifteen**. They were in charge not only of deciding the issue of allowing the Southern **congressmen** to participate but also of Reconstruction policies in general. They studied the problem for several months.

Thaddeus Stevens

When Congress did act, it passed a series of laws that changed the requirements for Southern states to be readmitted to the Union. Until those requirements were met, the Radical Republicans had a valid reason for refusing to allow Southern congressmen to participate.

To further strengthen their position, the Radicals added Section 3 to the Fourteenth Amendment, prohibiting anyone who had held office or been a leader of the Confederacy from voting or being elected.

Name: _____ Date: _____

Southern Congressmen Turned Away (cont.)

Directions: Complete the following exercises.

Matching

_____ 1. implement

_____ 2. Radical Republicans

_____ 3. Thaddeus Stevens

_____ 4. Committee of Fifteen

_____ 5. congressmen

a. leader of the Committee of Fifteen

b. to put into place

c. a committee of Radical Republicans who were in charge of deciding whether Southern congressmen would be allowed to participate in Congress

d. disqualified the Southern congressmen from serving

e. members of the Senate or the House of Representatives

Fill in the Blanks

1. He quickly readmitted all the former Confederate states except _____ to the Union.

2. The number of members a state has in the U.S. House of Representatives is based on _____.

3. Although it was dishonest and unfair, _____ _____ disqualified the Southern congressmen; then they appointed a committee to study the matter.

4. When Congress did act, it passed a series of _____ that changed the requirements for Southern states to be _____ to the Union.

5. Section 3 to the Fourteenth Amendment prohibited anyone who had held office or been a leader of the _____ from voting or being elected.

Critical Thinking

What do you think of the tactic used by the Radical Republicans in forming the Committee of Fifteen? Give specific details or examples to support your opinion.

_____

_____

_____

_____

_____

_____

_____

Name: _____ Date: _____

The Civil Rights Act of 1866

In March 1866, Congress passed another bill called the **Civil Rights Act**. This bill gave freedmen their civil rights and promised protection of their rights. It conferred citizenship upon black men and guaranteed them equal rights with whites.

Again President Johnson vetoed the bill. For the second time, Congress overrode Johnson's veto, making the bill a law in April 1866.

When Johnson learned that Congress had overridden his veto, he claimed that Congress was filled with traitors. Congress, led by Northern Radicals, came up with their own plan for Reconstruction.

Thaddeus Stevens, a leader of the Radical Republicans, stated: "Every man, no matter what his race or color … has an equal right to justice, honesty, fair play with every other man; and the law should secure him those rights …"

Although the Civil Rights Act granted citizenship and civil rights to black men, Congress felt it was necessary to make the law even stronger by writing another amendment to the Constitution in June. They sent it to the states for approval.

President Johnson publicly attacked this amendment and convinced all the former Confederate states, except Tennessee, to reject it. Delaware and Kentucky also failed to approve it. His actions caused a two-year delay before the amendment was finally approved. In the meantime, the gulf between the president and Congress grew wider.

The situation in the South grew worse. Violence increased. A white mob in Memphis, Tennessee, killed 47 blacks and destroyed homes, schools, and churches. During a political meeting of blacks in New Orleans, a mob of white policemen and firemen attacked the demonstrators. Most of the 48 people killed were blacks.

Constructed Response

What did the Civil Rights Act give to freedmen?

_____

_____

_____

_____

Name: _____ Date: _____

The Congressional Plan

Lincoln and Johnson's plans for Reconstruction were much more lenient than the plan proposed by Congress, which involved reorganizing the Southern states, setting provisions for readmitting them into the Union, and working out a system by which whites and blacks could live together in a nonslave society.

Congress declared that a majority of white male citizens had to swear that they had never been disloyal to the United States.

Congress also demanded that the states would have to ratify the Fourteenth Amendment and rewrite state constitutions abolishing slavery and making secession illegal.

Northerners that supported the congressional plan were called Radicals. They claimed that the South should not be permitted to get away with treason. Lincoln had not approved of the harsh measures and had refused to sign the plan into law.

The debate was fierce, but Congress finally gained enough power to implement its plan. Congress passed a series of Reconstruction Acts dividing the South into five military districts to be in effect until the states adopted new constitutions and were readmitted to the Union. The military presence ensured that blacks could vote without fear, and many even held political office for a short time.

Little was done to restore the South to its former economic status. As a result, the South lagged behind the North technologically, economically, and socially for many decades.

Southern whites were outraged and humiliated by Northern military rule. They refused to accept former slaves as equals. Most people in the South saw Reconstruction as a shameful, even vengeful, imposition.

Did You Know?

"Forty Acres and a Mule" was an expression that came to symbolize the expectations of newly freed slaves based on promises that Congress would divide up Southern estates and give them to former slaves. The expression came to mean any expectations that were unreasonable.

True or False

Directions: Write "T" if the statement is true or "F" if it is false.

1. T F Lincoln and Johnson's plan for Reconstruction was more harsh than the Congressional plan.

2. T F Southerners that supported the Congressional plan were called Radicals.

3. T F Lincoln refused to sign the Congressional plan into law.

4. T F The Congressional plan divided the South in to six military districts.

5. T F The South lagged behind the North technologically, economically, and socially for many decades.

Name: _____ Date: _____

The Fourteenth Amendment

Amendment 14

Section 1. All persons born or naturalized in the United States, and subject to the jurisdiction thereof, are citizens of the United States and of the state wherein they reside. No state shall make or enforce any law which shall abridge the privileges or immunities of citizens of the United States; nor shall any state deprive any person of life, liberty, or property, without due process of law; nor deny to any person within its jurisdiction the equal protection of the laws.

Adopted on July 28, 1868, the Fourteenth Amendment granted citizenship to men over 21 who had been born or naturalized in the United States. It also guaranteed **due process** (right to a trial by a jury) and equal protection under the law to all citizens.

However, even though the amendment said "all persons," it didn't mean everyone. Women and Native Americans were excluded. The exception for Native Americans is included in another section of the amendment, and the specific words "male citizens" are used to exclude women. This meant that women and Native Americans were not considered citizens and had none of the rights granted by the amendment.

Section 3 of this amendment banned everyone who formerly held office in one of the states that seceded from the Union during the Civil War from voting or holding public office. This section was designed to punish the leaders of the Confederacy and was not deleted by Congress until 1889.

The last part of Section 4 addresses the issue of repayment to slave-holders for their slaves.

. . . neither the United States nor any states shall assume or pay any debt or obligation incurred in aid of insurrection or rebellion against the United States, or any claim for the loss of emancipation of any slave, but all such debts, obligations, and claims shall be held illegal and void.

Constructed Response

Why were Native Americans and women not granted rights under the Fourteenth Amendment? Give specific details or examples to support your answer.

_____

_____

_____

_____

_____

UNIT THREE: RECONSTRUCTION

Name: _____ Date: _____

Reactions in the North

When the Civil War ended, Union soldiers were glad to return to their homes and families. Many had strong feelings against the South, especially during the first few months after the war.

Some had personal reasons, like the loss of loved ones. Different people in the North had different opinions. Some of the more common ones included these:

- The Southerners had started the war in the first place by seceding from the Union, so it was all their fault.

- Rebel soldiers had killed and wounded hundreds of thousands of Northern soldiers and should be made to pay for their crimes.

- The war had cost the country millions of dollars. The South should repay the North for the cost of the war.

- The lives of millions of Northerners had been disrupted for four years while the Civil War was fought.

Lincoln's funeral procession through New York City

- Southerners did not have the right to force people into slavery. Blacks should have equal rights.

Some Northerners wanted Southerners to pay for what they believed were crimes of treason. When Andrew Johnson pardoned former Confederate leaders, some Northerners were enraged. They believed the leaders, and possibly everyone who fought in the Confederate Army, should be imprisoned or hanged.

Critical Thinking

Select one of the reasons why Northerners wanted revenge on the South even after the war was over. Do you think they were right or wrong? Give specific details or examples to support your answer.

_____

_____

_____

_____

_____

_____

Name: _____ Date: _____

Reactions in the South

Southerners had many reasons for being angry after the Civil War ended.

- Hundreds of thousands of Confederate soldiers had died and been wounded. Many were permanently disabled.

- The Southern states believed that since they had joined the Union voluntarily, they had the right to leave it if they wished to do so.

- Slaves were property. The Constitution guaranteed men the right to own property. The government did not have the right to deprive them of their property.

- The North refused to mind its own business. The war was all its fault.

- The South had been defeated in the war.

- Much of the land, crops, and property in the South had been destroyed.

- The North forced Southerners to live under military rule during Reconstruction.

- Southerners were expected to treat blacks, whom they considered inferior beings, like equals.

In retaliation, many Southerners formed vigilante groups—secret terrorist organizations, such as the Ku Klux Klan and the Knights of the White Camelia—for the purpose of re-establishing white authority over blacks.

The Ku Klux Klan (KKK) and other similar groups intimidated blacks and other ethnic and religious minorities through threats and violence. Dressed in robes and masks to conceal their identities, they attacked government officials sent from the North and made night raids to terrorize blacks.

Critical Thinking

Select one of the reasons why Southerners felt angry and vengeful against Northerners. Do you think they were right or wrong? Give specific details or examples to support your answer.

_____

_____

_____

_____

_____

_____

UNIT THREE: RECONSTRUCTION

The Reconstruction Acts

To launch its new Reconstruction plan, Congress passed the first Reconstruction Act on March 2, 1867, in spite of President Johnson's veto.

The Act **nullified** all Southern state governments and divided the Confederacy into five military districts, each ruled by a military governor appointed by Congress.

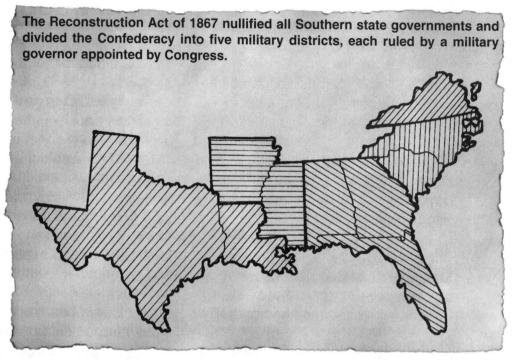

The Reconstruction Act of 1867 nullified all Southern state governments and divided the Confederacy into five military districts, each ruled by a military governor appointed by Congress.

"The whole fabric of Southern society must be changed," stated Thaddeus Stevens. The Act stated that the Southern states were to remain under federal military control until they were readmitted to the Union.

The Reconstruction Act also called for new state elections. Former Confederates were not allowed to vote or hold office. To ensure that blacks were permitted to vote, Union soldiers were sent into the South to maintain law and order. In spite of **resistance** by whites, 16 freedmen were elected to Congress.

Rather than accepting the **provisions** of the first Reconstruction Act and rewriting their constitutions, most Southern states ignored the law. No attempts were made to change their state constitutions or to reapply for **admission** to the Union.

For this reason, Congress passed three additional Reconstruction Acts. President Johnson vetoed each one, but they were passed anyway.

The Reconstruction Act of March 1867 allowed military commanders to control registration and voting. They could force states to call conventions to revise the state constitutions to **conform** with federal requirements. As a result, many freedmen were elected to local offices and became active members of the conventions.

The third Reconstruction Act passed in July added a provision that the Fifteenth Amendment must be ratified before the Southern states could be readmitted to the Union.

However, the Fifteenth Amendment and the new state constitutions had to be ratified by a majority of registered voters. To prevent this, Southerners simply refused to vote.

Congress passed a fourth Reconstruction Act in March 1868 stating that a majority of the votes actually cast would decide the adoption or rejection of a state constitution.

Name: _____ Date: _____

The Reconstruction Acts (cont.)

Directions: Complete the following exercises.

Matching

_____ 1. nullified

_____ 2. resistance

_____ 3. provisions

_____ 4. admission

_____ 5. conform

a. a measure taken beforehand to deal with a need

b. being allowed entry

c. to make legally null and void

d. to be obedient and compliant

e. the force exerted in opposition

Fill in the Blanks

1. To launch its new Reconstruction plan, _____ passed the first Reconstruction Act on March 2, 1867, in spite of President Johnson's veto.

2. "The whole fabric of Southern society must be changed," stated _____

   _____.

3. To ensure that blacks were permitted to vote, _____ soldiers were sent into the _____ to maintain law and order.

4. As a result, many _____ were elected to local offices and became active members of the conventions.

5. However, the _____ Amendment and the new state constitutions had to be ratified by a majority of registered voters.

Cause and Effect

Directions: A **cause** is an event that produces a result. An **effect** is the result produced. For each statement below, write a cause or effect.

1. **Cause:** _____

   _____

   Effect: The Act nullified all Southern state governments and divided the Confederacy into five military districts, each ruled by a military governor appointed by Congress.

2. **Cause:** The third Reconstruction Act added a provision that the Fifteenth Amendment must be ratified before the Southern states could be readmitted to the Union

   Effect: _____

   _____

3. **Cause:** The Reconstruction Act of March 1867 allowed military commanders to control registration and voting.

   Effect: _____

   _____

Name: _____ Date: _____

The Tenure of Office Act

Although President Johnson vetoed the bill, Congress passed the Tenure of Office Act on March 2, 1867.

The Tenure of Office Act denied the president the power to remove anyone from office who had been appointed with the consent of the Senate unless the Senate agreed.

Radical Republicans hoped that this would prevent President Johnson from replacing Secretary of War Edwin Stanton, who favored their Reconstruction Plan.

Edwin Stanton

Cabinet members are appointed by the president and approved by Congress. Their job is to act as advisors to the president.

President Johnson claimed that the act was unconstitutional because it interfered with the executive powers of the president included in the Constitution.

In August 1867, Johnson fired Edwin Stanton and appointed Ulysses S. Grant in his place. Grant had ambitions to run for president in the next election. He was warned that he might lose his chance to be nominated if he continued as secretary of war.

Grant resigned after five months and returned the position to Edwin Stanton, who barricaded himself in his office in the War Department. Johnson ordered his removal and appointed General Lorenzo Thomas to the position.

Congress began impeachment proceedings against President Johnson to have him removed from office. His violation of the Tenure of Office Act was the main charge against him.

Most of the Tenure of Office Act was repealed 20 years later. In 1926, the Supreme Court declared the act unconstitutional.

True or False

Directions: Write "T" if the statement is true or "F" if it is false.

1. T   F   Cabinet members are appointed by the president and approved by the Senate.

2. T   F   President Johnson passed the Tenure of Office Act on March 2, 1867.

3. T   F   Congress began impeachment proceedings against President Johnson, charging him with the violation of the Tenure of Office Act.

4. T   F   Cabinet members are appointed as advisors to Congress.

5. T   F   President Johnson claimed that the Tenure of Office Act was unconstitutional because it interfered with the executive powers of the president included in the Constitution.

Name: _____ Date: _____

The Fifteenth Amendment

Although the Fourteenth Amendment gave black men all rights of citizenship, many blacks were denied those rights, particularly the right to vote. Congress felt it was necessary to add another amendment that very specifically stated that all citizens had the right to vote and that no state could deny that right.

In many Southern states, particularly in Louisiana and Georgia, illegal methods were used to prevent former slaves from voting. Many were "disqualified" as voters by local officials. Terrorism by groups like the Ku Klux Klan frightened many potential black voters and kept them away from the polls.

Amendment 15

Section 1. The right of citizens of the United States to vote shall not be denied or abridged by the United States or by any state on account of race, color, or previous condition of servitude.

Proposed in February 1869, the Fifteenth Amendment was ratified in March of the following year. Section 2 gave Congress the right to make laws to enforce this amendment.

Since the Fourteenth Amendment defined citizens as males over the age of 21 except for Native Americans, the right to vote was still denied to women. Women's **suffrage**, (the right to vote) became a major issue during Reconstruction and was not finally resolved until the Nineteenth Amendment was passed in 1920.

Many places in the South ignored the amendments and continued to prevent blacks from exercising their rights. As late as 1965, Congress still felt it necessary to pass the Voting Rights Act.

Graphic Organizer Directions: Compare the Fourteenth and Fifteenth Amendments. On a separate piece of paper, create and complete a Venn diagram like the one shown.

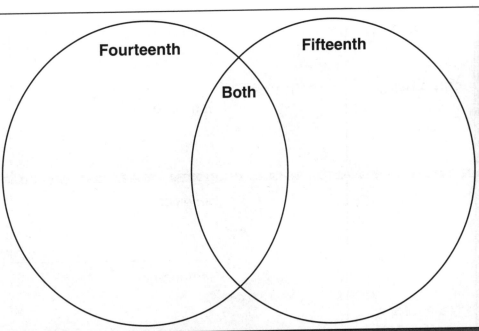

Fourteenth

Fifteenth

Both

UNIT THREE: RECONSTRUCTION

Name: _____ Date: _____

Carpetbaggers

Government agents, politicians, businessmen, adventurers, and others from the North who traveled to the South during Reconstruction were called **carpetbaggers**.

The name came to be used because people who traveled often carried their belongings in carpetbags. Carpetbags were similar to today's sports bags—soft-sided suitcases, made of carpeting with wooden handles.

Some carpetbaggers were representatives of the Freedmen's Bureau and other federal Reconstruction agencies. They were not well received by white Southerners.

Many of the people who became active in the South during Reconstruction included black and white teachers from the North and South and people from missionary organizations, churches, and schools. Their goal was to improve living conditions and to promote education for the freedmen.

Others were opportunists, looking for ways to exploit the political and financial problems of the South for their own gain. Because Congress banned all former Confederate leaders and soldiers from voting or holding public office for a time, carpetbaggers were often able to get elected.

Some carpetbaggers benefitted financially or politically during Reconstruction. Many others were able to improve education, provide medical assistance, and help restore Southern cities. Southerners who cooperated with carpetbaggers were called **scalawags**.

Graphic Organizer

Directions: Complete the vocabulary chart by creating a definition, using the word in a sentence, and drawing an illustration that helps you remember the meaning of each word.

Word	Definition	Illustration
carpetbaggers		
	Sentence	

Word	Definition	Illustration
scalawags		
	Sentence	

Name: _____ Date: _____

The Impeachment of the President

On February 24, 1868, the House of Representatives voted 126 to 47 to impeach Andrew Johnson for "high crimes and misdemeanors." Eleven charges were brought against Johnson. Eight of the charges were for violating the Constitution.

Johnson would now have to stand trial in the Senate to see if he would be removed from office. No U.S. President had ever been impeached before.

Johnson exploded when he heard the news. "Damn them! Haven't I been struggling ever since I have been in this chair to uphold the Constitution they trample underfoot!"

The trial began on March 23, 1868. Day after day evidence was presented and witnesses called. The case against the president was weak, based more on hatred and emotion than on fact. Johnson was represented by lawyers and did not attend the trial.

On May 7, 1868, the 54 members of the Senate on the jury began to weigh the evidence. They needed a two-thirds majority—36 votes—for a conviction. If only 35 voted guilty, Johnson would be acquitted.

The decisions of all members of the jury except one were known in advance. Senator Edmund Ross of Kansas remained undecided. The Radical Republicans put pressure on him and even attempted to bribe him.

On May 16, each member of the jury was asked how he voted. Senator Ross's vote was critical. One more vote was needed for a majority to convict the president and remove him from office.

Although he knew his political career would probably be over, Senator Ross voted not guilty. By a margin of one vote, the president was not convicted.

Andrew Johnson finished out his term as president. He and Congress continued to be at odds. Johnson continued to veto bills he thought were unfair.

"Everyone misunderstands me," Johnson claimed. "I am not trying to introduce anything new. I am only trying to carry out the measures towards the South that Mr. Lincoln would have done, had he lived."

Research

Directions: Two presidents have been impeached by Congress. Learn more about them. Use the information to complete the chart below.

President	Year	Charges	Results

Name: _____ Date: _____

Ulysses S. Grant

When Lincoln called for volunteers to put down the "rebellion" in the South, Ulysses S. Grant was a 39-year-old clerk living in Galena, Illinois.

Ulysses S. Grant

Grant, a graduate of West Point with fifteen years of soldiering experience, decided to volunteer. "I thought I had done with soldiering. I never expected to be in military life again. But … if my knowledge and experience can be of any service, I think I ought to offer them."

Grant drilled other Galena volunteers and marched with them to Springfield. He wrote to the War Department requesting a military commission. His letter wasn't answered. When he went to Cincinnati to meet George McClellan, the General refused to see him.

About to return to Galena, Grant received word from the governor of Illinois offering him command of the Twenty-Fourth Illinois Volunteer Regiment and the rank of colonel.

Grant proved himself a good officer. President Lincoln promoted him to Brigadier General. After his success in southern Illinois, Grant was sent to attack Confederate strongholds in Tennessee.

Grant became commander of the U.S. Army in the West following further victories. Under his leadership, the Union Army continued successful campaigns into the South, including the capture of Vicksburg, Mississippi.

In March 1864, President Lincoln put Grant in charge of the entire Union Army. His goal was to capture the Confederate capital at Richmond, Virginia. With 118,000 troops, Grant directed the army south.

During fierce battles, thousands were killed. After a siege of many months, Confederate General Robert E. Lee ordered a retreat. Finally on April 9, 1865, Lee surrendered to Grant near the village of Appomattox Court House, Virginia.

Learning that the Confederate troops had run out of food, Grant ordered supplies sent to them. When Union troops began loud celebrations, Grant ordered them to stop. "The war is over, the rebels are our countrymen again."

Critical Thinking

Why do you think Grant did not let the Union troops celebrate loudly? Give specific details or examples to support your answer.

_____

_____

_____

_____

_____

Name: _____ Date: _____

The Election of 1868

Other than the few months as the secretary of war under President Johnson, Ulysses S. Grant had never held any political office. In fact, he had never run for an election at any level.

When the Republican Convention met in 1868 to nominate a candidate for president, every delegate voted for Grant on the first ballot. Grant's running mate was Speaker of the House Schuyler Colfax of Indiana.

The Democrats nominated the governor of New York, Horatio Seymour, and Francis P. Blair of Missouri was chosen as his running mate.

During the presidential campaign, the Democrats attacked the Reconstruction plan and blacks' right to vote. They accused Grant of being a military despot and anti-Semitic. His running mate was accused of possible corruption.

The Republicans criticized Seymour's support for inflationary paper currency, Blair's reputed drunkenness, and Democratic opposition to Reconstruction.

Grant did not participate in the campaign. He remained at his home in Galena, Illinois, until the election results were known. Grant won the popular vote by 300,000 and earned 214 of the 294 electoral votes.

Many blacks voted for the first time in that presidential election. Former Confederates, mostly Democrats, were denied the right to vote. These two circumstances helped Grant win.

In his inauguration address, Grant urged ratification of the Fifteenth Amendment and expressed concern for proper treatment of Native Americans. He felt that they, too, should be citizens and allowed to vote.

Graphic Organizer
Directions: During the 1868 presidential campaign, each side attacked the other's candidate. Complete the chart listing the criticisms made by both political parties.

Democratic Criticism of Grant and Colfax	Republican Criticism of Seymour and Blair

Name: _____ Date: _____

President Grant's First Term

When Grant became president, he inherited many problems. Northern Republicans and Southern Democrats were still bitter rivals. Grant's lack of political experience soon became apparent. He appointed many personal and army friends to important positions.

Many of Grant's friends also lacked political experience and skills for the positions they received. Grant wasn't the first president to practice **nepotism**, or favoring friends and family. Most civil service jobs were by appointment—from cabinet members to postmasters in small towns. Grant's loyalty was praised, but he was often criticized for his poor judgment.

As the states were readmitted to the Union, federal troops were withdrawn. The Fifteenth Amendment did grant black men the right to vote; however, without federal protection, they were soon denied that right as well as many other civil rights in the South.

Terrorism and violence grew in the South. The **Ku Klux Klan Act of 1871** gave Grant the authority to investigate and prosecute crimes. Over 1,000 men were convicted of terrorism.

William Seward, the man who negotiated the purchase of Alaska from Russia, proposed a plan for the **Dominican Republic** to become part of the United States. Grant was convinced that this was a good idea. The land was rich and had many mineral resources, an ideal place for settlements of newly freed slaves. However, in spite of his strong support, Congress voted against the plan.

Another embarrassment to Grant occurred when two stock investors, Jay Gould and Jim Fisk, tried to corner the gold market by buying up gold to drive up the price. They pretended to be Grant's friends and convinced him not to sell any of the federal reserves of gold.

> **Did You Know?**
> President Grant was once arrested while he was president and fined $20 for exceeding the speed limit. He was riding his horse at the time.

When Grant realized what they were doing, he ordered $4 million in federal gold sold. That immediately lowered the price of gold and ruined **Fisk and Gould's scheme**, but it also caused financial ruin for many honest gold investors.

Graphic Organizer

Directions: Complete the chart below. Describe each of the events.

Event	Description
1. **Fisk and Gould's Scheme**	
2. **Dominican Republic Plan**	
3. **Ku Klux Klan Act of 1871**	

Name: _____ Date: _____

The Election of 1872

Near the end of Grant's first term as president, several important members of Congress were mixed up in a scandal involving stolen funds from the transcontinental railroad. Grant's vice president, Schuyler Colfax, and other government officials were accused of taking bribes.

Grant was not accused of any wrongdoing in the affair, and his popularity remained high. Again, he was nominated on the first ballot at the National Republican Convention. They did select a new running mate for his vice president, Senator Henry Wilson of Massachusetts.

Liberal Republicans decided to choose their own candidates. They nominated Horace Greeley, editor of the *New York Times,* and Governor B. Gratz Brown of Missouri. The Democrats supported Greeley also.

The campaign was filled with **mud-slinging**—personal accusations and insults against candidates. Political cartoons and insulting newspaper stories against Greeley were met with accusations of dishonesty, drunkenness, and stupidity against Grant.

Greeley supported civil service reform, a less radical approach to the South, and the end of Reconstruction. He toured the country giving speeches. At that time, it was unusual for a candidate to campaign for himself. Speeches were given by others but not by the candidates themselves.

The Republicans also called for civil service reform plus protection of blacks' rights. Grant, knowing he was not a good public speaker, remained at the family home during the campaign. Grant won the popular vote by an overwhelming majority.

Fill in the Blanks

1. Grant's vice president during his first term in office was _____

   _____.

2. Greeley, the candidate running against Grant, supported the end of

   _____.

3. In the election of 1872, Grant won the popular vote by an overwhelming

   _____.

4. _____ toured the country, giving campaign speeches, but

   _____, knowing he was not a good public speaker, remained at the family

   home during the campaign.

5. _____ _____ _____ of Massachusetts was

   selected as Grant's running mate.

6. The campaign was filled with personal accusations and insults called _____.

Name: _____ Date: _____

Grant's Second Term as President

The *New York Tribune* described Grant's speech when he began his second term of office as "the utterances of a man of the best intentions profoundly desirous to govern wisely and justly and profoundly ignorant of the means of which good government is secured."

That prediction proved to be true as problem after problem plagued Grant's administration. A severe drop in stock prices caused the Panic of 1873. Many banks failed and factories closed. The country faced a major economic depression.

Grant was unaware that he had appointed unscrupulous men to work in his administration. They accumulated fortunes by selling business contracts, padding government payrolls, committing fraud, and taking bribes.

Another scandal involved officials of the Treasury Department responsible for collecting taxes on liquor. Known as the "Whiskey Ring," they failed to turn over some of the money they collected.

Mrs. Grant wanted to have her sons closer to her. At her request, Grant appointed two of them as his personal secretaries. Again, people charged Grant with nepotism.

Ulysses S. Grant

As his second term came to an end, Grant decided not to run again. (At that time there was no restriction on the number of terms for the president.)

In his final State of the Union speech to Congress he said, "It was my fortune, or misfortune, to be called to the office of Chief Executive without any previous political training. Under such circumstances, it is but reasonable to suppose that errors of judgment must have occurred."

Grant did help the country survive the Reconstruction Era. He was the first president to try to help Native Americans and the first to use arbitration to solve international conflicts. He endorsed the Fifteenth Amendment and convinced Congress to pass the Ku Klux Klan Act, designed to protect the rights of blacks.

Graphic Organizer

Directions: Grant had no political training to prepare him for the presidency. Using the information from the reading exercise, classify the decisions he made by completing the chart below.

Contributions	Errors in Judgment

Name: _____ Date: _____

The Disputed Election of 1876

Although Ulysses S. Grant had been a popular president, his two terms of office were marred by scandals of bribery and corruption of public officials.

Since Grant had stated that he did not want to run for a third term, the Republicans nominated Rutherford B. Hayes. A moderate Republican, Hayes was not associated with any of the corruption of the Grant administration.

He too was a war hero, having risen to the rank of general and been wounded in the Civil War. Hayes was known for his honesty. As governor of Ohio, he had worked for civil rights for blacks.

The Democrats nominated Samuel Tilden, governor of New York. He also had a reputation for honesty. He was backed by many wealthy businessmen.

The election was close. When the votes were counted, Tilden had received 250,000 more votes than Hayes.

Presidential elections are not based on popular vote, however. The deciding factor is the number of electoral votes each candidate receives. Each state has a specific number of electoral votes, based on its population. To win the election, one candidate must have a majority of the electoral votes.

The Democrats claimed that votes from three Southern states (South Carolina, Florida, and Louisiana) had been falsely counted, and Tilden should have received those electoral votes. Both sides had used dirty tactics in the election, and both sides claimed victory in all three states. The electoral votes from those three states would decide the outcome of the election.

Congress set up an electoral commission of seven Republicans, seven Democrats, and Supreme Court Justice David Davis to settle the matter. Davis resigned from the commission and was replaced by a Republican. The committee gave the electoral votes of all three disputed states to Hayes, making him the winner 185 to 184.

Constructed Response

In the presidential election of 1876, Samuel Tilden received 250,000 more votes than Rutherford B. Hayes. Explain how Hayes became the president. Give specific details or examples to support your answer.

_____

_____

_____

_____

_____

_____

UNIT THREE: RECONSTRUCTION

Name: _____ Date: _____

Hayes Becomes President

Rutherford B. Hayes

As Inauguration Day approached, the Democrats threatened to prevent the votes from being counted, and the election was still in dispute. Finally, a plan known as the Compromise of 1877 was reached.

The Democrats agreed not to block Hayes from becoming president if Hayes would agree to withdraw the remaining troops from the South, name a Southerner to the Cabinet, and approve federal funds to rebuild the South.

In the 1800s, if Inauguration Day fell on a Sunday, the new president had to wait until Monday to be sworn in. That was the case in 1877.

Grant's term of office officially ended on Sunday, March 4. Hayes wasn't scheduled to be sworn in until Monday, March 5, but Grant didn't want to take any chances of the country being without a president, even for one day.

The Grants invited several people, including Rutherford B. Hayes, to a farewell dinner at the White House on Saturday, March 3. After dinner, Grant invited Hayes and Morrison Waite, Chief Justice of the Supreme Court, to the Red Room. There, in secret, Hayes took the oath of office.

Did You Know?

One of Hayes' nicknames was "Granny" Hayes because he didn't smoke, drink, or gamble. First Lady Lucy Hayes was known as "Lemonade" Lucy because she did not serve liquor in the White House—only lemonade.

Constructed Response

1. Explain how the Compromise of 1877 settled the election dispute. Give specific details or examples to support your answer.

   _____

   _____

   _____

   _____

2. Hayes was scheduled to be sworn into office on Monday, March 5. Explain why he took the oath of office on March 3 at the White House instead. Give specific details or examples to support your answer.

   _____

   _____

   _____

   _____

Jim Crow Laws and Segregation

The **Civil Rights Act of 1875** granted equal rights to blacks in public accommodations. It made **discrimination** based on color illegal in theaters, hotels, and on railroads and gave blacks the right to serve on juries.

However, that did not stop the South from passing **segregation** laws. The **"Jim Crow" laws** kept blacks and whites apart in public places like theaters, restaurants, hotels, schools, parks, trains, streetcars, and even restrooms and cemeteries.

"Jim Crow" was a character invented by Thomas Rice for a song-and-dance routine in which he impersonated an old, crippled slave. Minstrel shows were popular entertainment in the early to mid 1800s. White actors wore makeup to look like blacks, sang, danced, and told jokes, most of which made fun of slaves.

After Reconstruction (from 1877 thereafter), Southern states passed laws requiring separation of whites from **"persons of color"** in public transportation. Generally, anyone even suspected of having a black ancestor was considered a "person of color." Segregation not only separated the races, but it was also a way for whites to achieve **supremacy** over blacks.

Segregation was common in most public places and transportation. The goal of these laws was to prevent any contact between blacks and whites as equals.

Even the **Supreme Court** upheld the legality of Jim Crow Laws in a case in 1896, stating that segregation was legal if "separate, but equal" **facilities** were provided. (Most facilities were separate, but they were rarely equal.)

Laws were also passed to prevent blacks from voting by imposing a **poll tax**—a fee charged at the voting booth that was too expensive for most blacks to pay.

Many places also required voters to pass a **literacy test** to be eligible to vote. Since it had been illegal to educate slaves in the South, most adult freedmen could not read or write; therefore they could not vote.

Segregation was also practiced in the North. Although most states outlawed it after the Civil War, segregation was a reality in practice, if not in law.

Rather than getting more lax as time went on, the laws separating whites and blacks got stronger, and in some cases, very strange. For example, in some cities it was illegal for a black person to be within the city limits after sundown, and in Alabama, it was illegal for blacks and whites to play checkers together.

It took until 1954 for the Supreme Court to declare segregation in public schools unconstitutional. Some of the segregation laws remained in effect as late as 1964.

Name: _____ Date: _____

Jim Crow Laws and Segregation (cont.)

Directions: Complete the following exercises.

Matching

_____ 1. Civil Rights Act of 1875

_____ 2. segregation

_____ 3. "Jim Crow" laws

_____ 4. persons of color

_____ 5. supremacy

_____ 6. Supreme Court

_____ 7. poll tax

_____ 8. literacy test

_____ 9. discrimination

_____ 10. facilities

a. highest court in the land

b. a reading and writing test

c. anyone suspected of having a black ancestor

d. kept blacks and whites separate

e. dominance; authority; power

f. prejudice

g. granted equal rights to blacks in public accommodations

h. public accommodations: theaters, restaurants, hotels, schools, parks, trains, streetcars, and even restrooms

i. a fee charged at the voting booth

j. separate

Fill in the Blanks

1. "Jim Crow" was a character invented by Thomas Rice for a song-and-dance routine in which he impersonated an old, crippled _____.

2. After Reconstruction, Southern states passed laws requiring _____ of whites from "persons of color" in public transportation.

3. The goal of these laws was to prevent any contact between _____ and _____ as equals.

4. Since it had been illegal to educate slaves in the South, most adult freedmen could not read or write; therefore they could not _____.

5. It took until 1954 for the _____ _____ to declare segregation in public schools unconstitutional.

Technology in the Classroom
Primary Source: <http://ourdocuments.gov/doc.ph?flash=true&dpc=97>
("Civil Rights Act (1964)." Our Documents)

Directions: Before 1964, life in the United States did not provide equal opportunities for all citizens. The purpose of the Civil Rights Act of 1964 was to eliminate segregation, prejudice, and inequality. One minority affected by this act was African Americans. Research achievements made by African Americans since the passage of this act. Using the research, create a time line of these accomplishments.

Name: _____ Date: _____

Reconstruction: Success or Failure?

Was Reconstruction a success or a failure?

Some reasons why Reconstruction was a failure:

- In most places in the South, the rights granted to blacks by the amendments and Civil Rights laws were ignored.

- Violence against blacks increased.

- Although they legally had civil rights, in practice blacks, especially in the South, were not much better off than they had been as slaves. They were free in name only.

- The North failed to control the South and to change the basic attitude of Southerners towards blacks.

- Hard feelings between the North and South continued for many decades.

- The South continued to lag behind the North economically.

Some reasons why Reconstruction was a success:

- Three amendments were passed freeing slaves and giving them citizenship and the right to vote. At least in some parts of the country, blacks were allowed their rights.

- Two Civil Rights Acts gave blacks equality, at least in the eyes of the law.

- Even an unequal freedom was better than slavery.

- Although schools were segregated, and schools for blacks were often less well-funded, the laws against education for blacks had finally been repealed.

- Many people made a commitment to a society based on equality. Even though it did not become a reality during Reconstruction, the groundwork for future change and the Civil Rights movement of the twentieth century was established.

Research

Directions: Make a scrapbook about the Reconstruction Era. Add captions for all pictures. You can download pictures from the Internet, photocopy them from books, or draw your own.

Name: _____ Date: _____

Then and Now

Directions: Read the statements about conditions during Reconstruction. Add a statement about conditions today.

Then: In the early years after the Civil War, the Black Codes kept blacks in the South in conditions close to slavery.

Now: _____

_____

Then: Even though the Civil Rights Act of 1875 gave blacks equal rights in public places like hotels, trains, and theaters, they were seldom able to exercise those rights.

Now: _____

_____

Then: After they were free, blacks in the South were denied their rights. Even in the North, they faced much prejudice.

Now: _____

_____

Then: Andrew Johnson was President of the United States.

Now: _____

_____

Then: The Radical Republicans controlled Congress. They were engaged in what was almost an open war with the president.

Now: _____

_____

Then: Women and Native Americans were not considered citizens and were not allowed to vote.

Now: _____

_____

Name: _____ Date: _____

Reconstruction Word Search

Directions: Look up, down, backward, forward, and diagonally in the puzzle to find and circle the words listed below. The words are all associated with the Reconstruction era.

AMENDMENT	CARPETBAGGERS	DISCRIMINATION	ELECTION
EMANCIPATION	GRANT	HAYES	IMPEACH
INAUGURATION	JOHNSON	RATIFICATION	RECONSTRUCTION
RIGHTS	SCALAWAGS	SEGREGATION	SUPREMACY

```
D Z R A T I F I C A T I O N X C Z T
W M N H I N A U G U R A T I O N N L
R Q O J A N O S N H O J G B W E D N
K D I R Y Y Z L M L B G X X M G W F
T I T D F L E T T J M M J D T R D Y
P S A N R L H S F C L S N Z T E S B
L C G L O Z H C F B G E K Q Z C R B
Y R E X Z I G X I A M Z T J M O E S
V I R P H D T M W A T G N L Z N G U
K M G B H Z P A L G R A N T B S G P
C I E M F E L N P J F K V M M T A R
F N S T A A R O Q I M C P G Z R B E
T A R C C K B I N R C T Y L D U T M
V T H S Y N Z T X V I N G C X C E A
B I P H T R H C N K D G A N L T P C
G O V M N C J E N T M F H M C I R Y
F N L M P Y V L K Q N X T T E O A V
P T Y J Y M G E T M K C B F S N C L
```

Name: _____ Date: _____

Research Project

Directions: Learn more about one of the people listed below who had an impact on history during the Reconstruction Era. Use the information to create an illustrated time line of their life.

William Seward

Eliza McCardle Johnson

Francis P. Blair
B. Gratz Brown
Blanche K. Bruce
Schuyler Colfax
Kate Cumming
Frederick Douglass
W.E.B. DuBois
Oscar J. Dunn
William Evart
Nathan Forest
Jay Gould
Julia Dent Grant
Ulysses S. Grant
Horace Greeley
Lucy Webb Hayes
Rutherford B. Hayes
Oliver Howard
Julia Ward Howe
Andrew Johnson
Eliza McCardle Johnson
Abraham Lincoln
John W. Menard
Ely S. Parker
Joseph Hayne Rainey
Hiram R. Revels
Carl Schurz
William Seward
Horatio Seymour
Robert Smalls
Edwin Stanton
Thaddeus Stevens
Charles Sumner
Samuel Tilden
Benjamin Wade
Henry Wilson

Blanche K. Bruce

Julia Dent Grant

Answer Keys

(No answers are listed for activities where answers may vary.)

Unit One: Slavery

Slavery Time Line Activity (p. 2)

A. 7   B. 6   C. 2   D. 3   E. 5
F. 10   G. 8   H. 9   I. 1   J. 4

1. Jamestown
2. 1865
3. 1804
4. New York
5. France
6. William Lloyd Garrison
7. 1820
8. Fugitive Slave Act
9. 1857

A Historical View of Slavery (p. 4)
Matching
1. e   2. d   3. b   4. c   5. a
Fill in the Blanks
1. slaves
2. ten, Portuguese, Portugal
3. horses, silver
4. thousand
5. Jamestown

Europe and Slavery (p. 6)
Matching
1. c   2. e   3. a   4. b   5. d
Fill in the Blanks
1. Spain
2. Europe
3. Native
4. England
5. Hawkins, profit
Research
1. Americas   2. England   3. Americas
4. England   5. Americas   6. England
7. England   8. Americas   9. England
10. Africa   11. Americas   12. Africa
13. Americas   14. Africa   15. Americas

Life Aboard a Slave Ship (p. 8)
Matching
1. e   2. c   3. a   4. b   5. d
Fill in the Blanks
1. beaten, killed
2. imprisoned
3. 15, 25
4. Atlantic
5. five
Vocabulary
inhumane, terrifying, atrocious, cruel, filthy, dreadful

Slavery in the South (p. 11)
Matching
1. b   2. c   3. e   4. a   5. d
Fill in the Blanks
1. Southern
2. 25
3. 50
4. cotton
5. Eli Whitney

Slavery in the North (p. 12)
Constructed Response
Whites were afraid that they would lose their jobs to blacks and become unemployed. This led to mob violence. Many blacks fled to Canada. White rioters destroyed black churches, schools, and homes. They attacked black men and women on the streets.

Phillis Wheatley (p. 16)
Fill in the Blanks
1. slave traders
2. Boston
3. English, write
4. 17, England
5. free

The Fugitive Slave Laws (p. 18)
Matching
1. e   2. b   3. __   __. __   5. d
Fill in the Blanks
1. Canada
2. property
3. 1793
4. civil liberties
5. federal marshals
Constructed Response
1. made it mandatory for federal marshals to assist in recapturing runaway slaves
2. penalized anyone who helped a slave to escape

Graphic Organizer

Northerners: felt it violated civil liberties; believed that once a slave entered a free state, he or she should automatically be free; felt it didn't offer enough protection to free slaves

Southerners: felt the law wasn't strong enough as there were no penalties for helping a slave escape or for harboring a fugitive; believed the federal law violated the rights of states to make their own laws regarding property

Abolitionist Movement (p. 22)
Matching
1. d   2. b   3. e   4. c   5. a
Fill in the Blanks
1. America
2. newspapers, books
3. songs
4. peacefully
5. equal rights

Nat Turner (p. 23)
Constructed Response
When he was young, Nat's mother, as well as other slaves, believed he was a prophet with mysterious powers. As he grew, he believed his purpose in life was to free the slaves. He said he heard voices and had visions. After he was captured, he said he had a vision of white and black spirits "engaged in battle." A voice told him that this was his destiny and he was to bear the burden.

The Underground Railroad (p. 27)
Matching
1. e   2. b   3. d   4. a   5. c
Fill in the Blanks
1. paths, people
2. secret
3. black
4. Quakers
5. runaway slaves
Constructed Response
a major slave uprising and the escape of their slaves

The *Dred Scott* Decision (p. 33)
Matching
1. e   2. a   3. b   4. d   5. c
Fill in the Blanks
1. Virginia
2. freedom
3. Supreme Court
4. appealed
5. Taney, citizens

Frederick Douglass (p. 35)
Constructed Response
Slave owners believed it was more likely for educated slaves to try to escape.

First Name, Last Name (p. 37)
1. Abraham Lincoln
2. Dred Scott
3. Elizabeth Freeman
4. Frederick Douglass
5. Harriet Tubman
6. John Brown
7. Nat Turner
8. Phillis Wheatley
9. Sojourner Truth
10. Thomas Garrett
11. William Garrison

Word Search

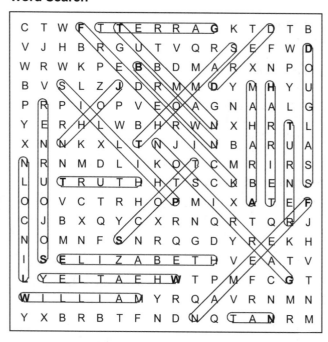

Unit Two: The Civil War

Civil War Time Line Activity (p. 40)
A. 8   B. 4   C. 2   D. 10   E. 3
F. 7   G. 1   H. 6   I. 9   J. 5

1. T   2. F   3. T   4. F   5. F

Abraham Lincoln (p. 42)

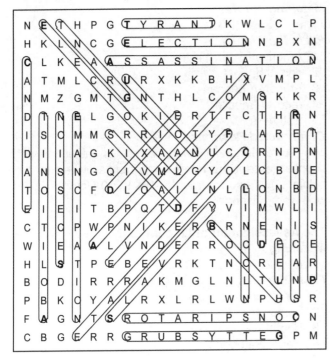

The Election of 1860 (p. 44)
Matching
1. e   2. c   3. a   4. b   5. d
Fill in the Blanks
1. slavery, states'
2. Abraham Lincoln
3. Stephen Douglas
4. radical, Democrats
5. Constitutional Unionists
Chart
1. 4,582,069
2. 39%
3. 30%
4. 59%
5. 4%

Causes of the Civil War (p. 47)
Graphic Organizer
Expansion: North wanted to end expansion; South wanted to extend to all new states

States' Rights: North believed federal government should have more power than individual states; South believed individual states should have more control over their laws than the federal government

The Union: North believed the United States must remain one country to remain strong; South claimed the United States was an organization of independent states—since they chose to join it, they could choose to leave it and form their own county

Tariffs: North wanted high tariffs; South did not want to pay tariffs

Jefferson Davis (p. 50)
1. Kentucky
2. Mississippi
3. Transylvania University in Kentucky
4. Zachary Taylor
5. Mississippi
6. to Congress
7. foot
8. Secretary of War
9. camels
10. Montgomery, Alabama
11. Robert E. Lee
12. Northerners

Abraham Lincoln or Jefferson Davis? (p. 51)
Research
1. JD   2. Both   3. AL   4. AL   5. AL
6. JD   7. JD   8. Both   9. AL   10. JD
11. AL   12. JD   13. JD   14. AL   15. JD

Who Started the Civil War? (p. 53)
Cause and Effect
1. Southern states seceded from the Union.
2. The South refused to abolish slavery.

Grant or Lee? (p. 55)
Research
1. LEE	2. GRANT	3. GRANT
4. LEE	5. GRANT	6. LEE
7. LEE	8. GRANT	9. GRANT
10. LEE	11. LEE	12. GRANT
13. GRANT	14. LEE	15. GRANT

The Glories of War (p. 57)
Research
Antietam—Date: September 17, 1862; State: Maryland; Casualties: North–2,108; South–1,546

Fort Sumter—Date: April 12–13, 1861; State: South Carolina; Casualties: North–0; South–0

The First Battle of Bull Run—Date: July 21, 1861; State: Virginia; Casualties: North–460; South–387

Battle of Fredericksburg—Date: December 11–15, 1862; State: Virginia; Casualties: North–1,284; South–608

Battle of Gettysburg—Date: July 1–3, 1863; State: Pennsylvania; Casualties: North–3,155; South–4,708

Battle of Lookout Mountain—Date: November 24, 1863; State: Tennessee; Casualties: North–408; South–187

Battle of Murfreesboro—Date: December 31, 1862 to January 2, 1863; State: Tennessee; Casualties: North–1,730; South–1,294

Battle of Pea Ridge—Date: March 6-8, 1862; State: Arkansas; Casualties: North–1,384; South–2,000

Battle of Shiloh—Date: April 6–8, 1862; State: Tennessee; Casualties: North–1,754; South–1,728

Siege of Vicksburg—Date: May 18 to July 4, 1863; State: Mississippi; Casualties: North–4,835; South–3,202

The War at Sea (p. 61)
True or False
1. T 2. F 3. T 4. F
5. F 6. T 7. T 8. T

Graphic Organizer
U.S.S. *Monitor*: North-built ironclad ship; U.S.S. *Monitor* sank in a storm

Both: ironclad ships used during the Civil War

C.S.S. *Virginia*: The South raised the sunken U.S.S. *Merrimac*, covered it in iron plating, and renamed it C.S.S. *Virginia*; crew destroyed the ship

Lincoln Issues the Emancipation Proclamation (p. 63)
Research
1. Fifteenth Amendment
2. 1870
3. Nineteenth Amendment
4. 1920

Black Soldiers Help Win the War (p. 65)
Matching
1. e 2. c 3. d 4. a 5. b
Fill in the Blanks
1. Revolutionary War
2. captain
3. territory, motives
4. 186,000; 400
5. Confederates
True or False
1. F 2. F 3. F 4. T 5. T
6. T 7. F 8. T 9. T 10. T

Lincoln's Gettysburg Address (p. 68)
Matching
1. e 2. a 3. d 4. b 5. c
Constructed Response
1. Lincoln's aim in his Gettysburg Address was to honor the people fighting for our nation who died in hope that there would still be a nation in the end.
2. Winning the war. The "great task ahead of us" was referring to ending the war, binding the nation's wounds, and bringing the South back into the Union.

The Civil War Ends (p. 70)
Matching
1. c 2. b 3. e 4. d 5. a
Fill in the Blanks
1. Americans
2. one-fifth
3. African-Americans
4. recover, rebuild
5. Southern
Constructed Response
Lee surrendered all men, arms, ammunition, and supplies except the horses and mules owned by the soldiers. He also returned about 1,000 Union soldiers who were prisoners of war.

The Assassination of Lincoln (p. 72)
Matching
1. a 2. e 3. c 4. d 5. b
Fill in the Blanks
1. John Parker
2. horse
3. Booth
4. Henry Rathbone
5. consciousness, died

Unit Three: Reconstruction

Reconstruction Time Line Activity (p. 78)
A. 12	B. 19	C. 2	D. 4	E. 1
F. 8	G. 7	H. 11	I. 3	J. 13
K. 9	L. 6	M. 18	N. 17	O. 5
P. 20	Q. 16	R. 15	S. 10	T. 14

Reconstruction (p. 80)
Matching
1. c 2. d 3. b 4. a 5. e
Fill in the Blanks
1. Confederate
2. South
3. social system
4. Reconstruction
5. disputes

Reconstruction Under President Johnson (p. 85)
Constructed Response
Johnson offered blacks no role in Reconstruction. He believed white men alone must manage the South.

The Black Codes of 1865 and 1866 (p. 86)
Constructed Response
A vagrant is a person unemployed and without a permanent residence.

Carl Schurz Reports to the President (p. 87)
Constructed Response
Former slaves: wanted to own homes, hold good jobs, and provide education for themselves and their children

Southerners: still viewed blacks as property, not people

How Congress Passes Laws (p. 89)
Fill in the Blanks
1. U.S. Constitution
2. bill
3. majority
4. ten
5. two-thirds

No Homes for the Homeless (p. 90)
Cause and Effect
1. Special Field Order No. 15 was issued by General Sherman.
2. helped homeless blacks find places to live
3. Southerners were pardoned and their land returned to them.

Southern Congressmen Turned Away (p. 92)
Matching
1. b   2. d   3. a   4. c   5. e
Fill in the Blanks
1. Texas
2. population
3. Radical Republicans
4. laws, readmitted
5. Confederacy

The Civil Rights Act of 1866 (p. 93)
Constructed Response
The Civil Rights Act gave freedmen their civil rights and promised to protect them. It conferred citizenship upon black men and guaranteed them equal rights with whites.

The Congressional Plan (p. 94)
True or False
1. F   2. F   3. T   4. F   5. T

The Fourteenth Amendment (p. 95)
Constructed Response
Native Americans were not considered citizens. The words "male citizens" were used to exclude women. The amendment granted citizenship to men over 21 years of age who had been born or naturalized in the United States.

The Reconstruction Acts (p. 99)
Matching
1. c   2. e   3. a   4. b   5. d
Fill in the Blanks
1. Congress
2. Thaddeus Stevens
3. Union, South
4. freedmen
5. Fifteenth
Cause and Effect
1. The first Reconstruction Act of 1867.
2. Southerners refused to vote.
3. Many freedmen were elected to local offices and became active members of the convention.

The Tenure of Office Act (p. 100)
True or False
1. T   2. F   3. T   4. F   5. T

The Fifteenth Amendment (p. 101)
Graphic Organizer
Fourteenth: gave black men all rights of citizenship
Both: Rights of black men
Fifteenth: citizens could not be denied the right to vote

The Impeachment of the President (p. 103)
Research
Andrew Johnson: 1868; violating the Constitution and the Tenure of Office Act; not guilty
William (Bill) Clinton; 1998–99; perjury, obstruction of justice, and malfeasance in office; not guilty

The Election of 1868 (p. 105)
Graphic Organizer
Democrats: Grant was accused of being a military despot and anti-Semitic; Colfax was accused of corruption
Republicans: Seymour was accused of supporting inflationary paper currency; Blair was accused of drunkenness; both accused of opposition to the Reconstruction plan

President Grant's First Term (p. 106)
Graphic Organizer
1. Tried to corner the gold market by buying up gold to drive up the price
2. Plan for the Dominican Republic to become part of the United States and a place for the settlement of newly freed slaves
3. Gave Grant authority to investigate and prosecute crimes of terrorism and violence in the South

The Election of 1872 (p. 107)
Fill in the Blanks
1. Schuyler Colfax
2. Reconstruction
3. .. majority
4. Greeley, Grant
5. Senator Henry Wilson
6. mudslinging

Grant's Second Term as President (p. 108)
Graphic Organizer
Contributions: First president to try to help Native Americans; first to use arbitration to solve international conflicts; endorsed the Fifteenth Amendment; convinced Congress to pass the Ku Klux Klan Act

Errors in Judgment: Appointed unscrupulous men to work in his administration; officials of the Treasury Department failed to turn over all money they collected; appointed sons as his personal secretaries

The Disputed Election of 1876 (p. 109)
Constructed Response
To win the election, a candidate must have a majority of the electoral votes. Hayes received 185 electoral votes and Tilden received 184. The electoral committee voted to give the disputed votes in three states to Hayes.

Hayes Becomes President (p. 110)
Constructed Response
1. Democrats agreed not to block Hayes from becoming president if Hayes would agree to withdraw the remaining troops from the South, name a Southerner to the Cabinet, and approve federal funds to rebuild the South.
2. Grant's term ended on Sunday. Hayes was scheduled to be sworn in on Monday. Grant didn't want the country to be without a president.

Jim Crow Laws and Segregation (p. 112)
Matching
1. g   2. j   3. d   4. c   5. e
6. a   7. i   8. b   9. f   10. h
Fill in the Blanks
1. slave
2. separation
3. blacks, whites
4. vote
5. Supreme Court

Reconstruction Word Search (p. 115)

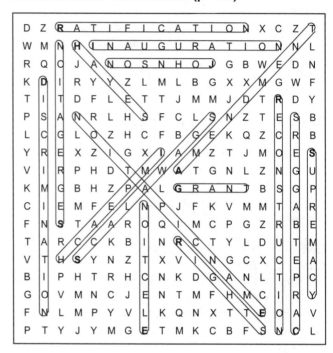